Application Testing with Capybara

Confidently implement automated tests for web applications using Capybara

Matthew Robbins

[PACKT] open source*
community experience distilled
PUBLISHING

BIRMINGHAM - MUMBAI

Application Testing with Capybara

First published: September 2013

Production Reference: 1160913

Published by Packt Publishing Ltd.
Livery Place
35 Livery Street
Birmingham B3 2PB, UK.

ISBN 978-1-78328-125-1

`www.packtpub.com`

Cover Image by VigilancePrime (`en.wikipedia`)

Credits

Author
Matthew Robbins

Reviewers
Yavor Atanasov
Graham Lyons
Daniel Morrison

Acquisition Editor
Aarthi Kumaraswamy

Commissioning Editor
Poonam Jain

Technical Editors
Hardik B. Soni
Krutika Parab

Copy Editors
Adithi Shetty
Sayanee Mukherjee
Alfida Paiva

Project Coordinator
Sherin Padayatty

Proofreaders
Clyde Jenkins
Christopher Smith

Indexer
Priya Subramani

Graphics
Ronak Dhruv

Production Coordinator
Arvindkumar Gupta

Cover Work
Arvindkumar Gupta

About the Author

Matthew Robbins is an experienced developer in test, having spent many years wrestling with commercially available test automation tools. He has spent the last five years immersed in developing robust test automation frameworks using open source tools. He worked extensively with the BBC developing test automation frameworks and tools across their web platform and continues to work in the media industry for other high-profile broadcasters. Aside from test automation, he is passionate about becoming more productive in Vim and learning about web browser internals. He also regularly blogs at `http://opensourcetester.co.uk`.

I would like to thank Catherine, Jared, and Leon, my wonderful family for all their support. Also huge thanks to the BBC Frameworks team especially Pete, Graham, and Yavor for starting me on this journey.

About the Reviewers

Yavor Atanasov is a software engineer who has in-depth experience within the whole spectrum of web development at a very large scale. He is from Bulgaria, currently living and working in London. He has seen the quirks of client-side JavaScript development and the importance of architecting and writing efficient backend systems. Agile practices, test-driven and behavior-driven approach to software development are all a fundamental part of his work. He has also experienced the complexity of acceptance testing sizeable multilayer systems.

Graham Lyons is a software engineer who has been working on the Web for around six years. Currently working on the platform at the BBC, he likes elegant, well-tested code, written in a variety of languages, and probably spends far too much time thinking about solutions to engineering problems. When he's not doing that, he enjoys fresh air and good coffee and is currently planning his wedding to a very patient lady.

Daniel Morrison is the founder of Collective Idea (`http://collectiveidea.com`), a software development consultancy in Holland, Michigan. At Collective Idea, Daniel has worked with Fortune 50 companies and built software for auto manufacturers, Silicon Valley startups, and everything in between. He writes a lot of web applications and teaches software development courses around the globe.

Table of Contents

Preface

One of my colleagues once described the Ruby community as "Test Infected" and if any library epitomizes this it's Capybara, which has gained popularity exponentially since it was first released. The Ruby community certainly owes its creator *Jonas Nicklas* a great deal of thanks for bringing peace and harmony to many test automation code bases around the globe.

The proof of Capybara's success is the way in which its use has spread far beyond just testing Rails applications and now supports testing of many web applications written in a wide variety of languages and frameworks. Capybara's functionality has also been replicated in languages other than Ruby again highlighting just how powerful the concept is.

So what is Capybara?

Capybara provides a domain-specific language for test automation; this DSL extends the human-readable BDD style of frameworks such as Cucumber and RSpec into the automation code itself. For example, opening a browser and navigating to a URL is as simple as `visit http://google.com`. This is a vast improvement over typical test APIs.

Additionally Capybara allows us to write tests once and run them in any compatible driver. The driver ecosystem is vibrant and switching libraries is as simple as adding an additional gem and making a one-line change to your code.

Finally, you can do away with writing bespoke methods that wait for content to become visible or adding sleep statements to your tests; Capybara handles asynchronous JavaScript without the user even noticing.

Capybara is quite literally your one-stop shop for test automation.

What this book covers

Chapter 1, Your First Scenario with Capybara, covers installation and configuration of your first scenario using Capybara.

Chapter 2, Mastering the API, provides a deep dive into Capybara's API for interacting with web pages.

Chapter 3, Testing Rails and Sinatra Applications, helps us explore how Capybara is particularly suited to testing applications implemented using Rails or Sinatra.

Chapter 4, Dealing with Ajax, JavaScript, and Flash, covers how to handle asynchronous JavaScript and how to use Capybara to test black box components such as Flash or HTML5 Canvas, Audio, and Video.

Chapter 5, Ninja Topics, helps us in using Capybara outside Cucumber in bespoke frameworks, within popular test frameworks such as RSpec and explores some alternatives to Capybara's built-in drivers.

What you need for this book

This book and the examples were developed using Ruby-1.9.3p237, RubyGems 1.8.23, and most importantly Capybara 2.1.0, which introduced some significant changes. All other dependencies will be downloaded by either RubyGems or Bundler when you install Capybara. We will also use Cucumber and RSpec, the latest versions of which should all be compatible with Capybara 2.1.0 and above.

Who this book is for

This book is for developers and testers who, with some exposure to Ruby, want to know how to test their applications using Capybara and its compatible drivers such as Selenium WebDriver and Rack::Test. The examples are deliberately kept simple and example HTML markup is always included so that readers can copy the examples to practice and experiment on their own machine.

Conventions

In this book, you will find a number of styles of text that distinguish between different kinds of information. Here are some examples of these styles, and an explanation of their meaning.

Code words in text, database table names, folder names, filenames, file extensions, pathnames, dummy URLs, user input, and Twitter handles are shown as follows: "The only source of confusion here might be the use of the string literal `search_query` in the `fill_in` method."

A block of code is set as follows:

```
<div id="main">
    <div class="section">
        <a id="myanchor" title="myanchortitle" href="#">Click this
           Anchor</a>
     </div>
</div>
```

Any command-line input or output is written as follows:

```
$ ruby -v
ruby 1.9.3p327 (2012-11-10 revision 37606) [x86_64-darwin11.4.2]
```

New terms and **important words** are shown in bold. Words that you see on the screen, in menus or dialog boxes for example, appear in the text like this: "After this we need to enter our search terms and click on the **Search** button."

[Warnings or important notes appear in a box like this.]

[Tips and tricks appear like this.]

Reader feedback

Feedback from our readers is always welcome. Let us know what you think about this book—what you liked or may have disliked. Reader feedback is important for us to develop titles that you really get the most out of.

To send us general feedback, simply send an e-mail to `feedback@packtpub.com`, and mention the book title via the subject of your message.

If there is a topic that you have expertise in and you are interested in either writing or contributing to a book, see our author guide on `www.packtpub.com/authors`.

Customer support

Now that you are the proud owner of a Packt book, we have a number of things to help you to get the most from your purchase.

Downloading the example code

You can download the example code files for all Packt books you have purchased from your account at `http://www.packtpub.com`. If you purchased this book elsewhere, you can visit `http://www.packtpub.com/support` and register to have the files e-mailed directly to you.

Errata

Although we have taken every care to ensure the accuracy of our content, mistakes do happen. If you find a mistake in one of our books—maybe a mistake in the text or the code—we would be grateful if you would report this to us. By doing so, you can save other readers from frustration and help us improve subsequent versions of this book. If you find any errata, please report them by visiting `http://www.packtpub.com/submit-errata`, selecting your book, clicking on the **errata submission form** link, and entering the details of your errata. Once your errata are verified, your submission will be accepted and the errata will be uploaded on our website, or added to any list of existing errata, under the Errata section of that title. Any existing errata can be viewed by selecting your title from `http://www.packtpub.com/support`.

Piracy

Piracy of copyright material on the Internet is an ongoing problem across all media. At Packt, we take the protection of our copyright and licenses very seriously. If you come across any illegal copies of our works, in any form, on the Internet, please provide us with the location address or website name immediately so that we can pursue a remedy.

Please contact us at `copyright@packtpub.com` with a link to the suspected pirated material.

We appreciate your help in protecting our authors, and our ability to bring you valuable content.

Questions

You can contact us at `questions@packtpub.com` if you are having a problem with any aspect of the book, and we will do our best to address it.

1
Your First Scenario with Capybara

Capybara brings two key ingredients to test automation: human-readable code via an elegant **domain-specific language** (**DSL**) and the ability to write once and run on multiple drivers such as **Selenium WebDriver** or **Rack::Test** for Rails/Sinatra applications. Through the course of this book we will see how Capybara can greatly increase the resilience of our tests and enhance our productivity.

In this chapter we will walk through installing Capybara and get up and running straight away with a simple scenario.

Specifically, we will cover the following:

- Ensuring that Ruby, RubyGems, and Bundler are available
- Ensuring that you have the necessary system libraries available
- Installing the Capybara gem
- Implementing your first scenario with Capybara, Cucumber, and Selenium WebDriver

Installing Capybara

Installing Capybara is no different than installing any other Ruby gem; if you have done any Ruby development in the past, it is likely that you will have all the prerequisites, and this process will be straightforward.

Preparing your system

Capybara is a Ruby gem and as such we need to ensure Ruby is available on the system.

> When you are learning a new library, it makes sense to use standard Ruby (as opposed to Ruby that runs on a different platform, such as JRuby or Iron Ruby) and run everything from the command line. This simply limits the amount of things that might go wrong due to the quirks of a less well-supported platform or an overly complicated IDE.

Open a command prompt and check the version of your Ruby interpreter:

```
$ ruby -v
ruby 1.9.3p327 (2012-11-10 revision 37606) [x86_64-darwin11.4.2]
```

If you see anything greater than 1.9, perfect! This means the correct version of Ruby installed and available for you to use.

If you see `command not found`, this means either Ruby is not installed or the system cannot find it. If you think you have installed Ruby, try modifying your `PATH` variable and add the location of the Ruby executable.

If you see anything less than 1.9, you should upgrade your current version of Ruby to 1.9 or greater. Capybara has a lot of dependencies and it no longer supports versions of Ruby prior to 1.9.

Installing gems with RubyGems

Like most languages Ruby has its own mechanism for managing libraries of code. **RubyGems** is the software used to manage gems that are libraries and Capybara is a Ruby gem itself.

The RubyGems application typically gets installed when you first install Ruby but it is worth double-checking if you have it.

At your command prompt, check the version of RubyGems installed by running the following command:

```
$ gem -v
1.8.23
```

If you see anything greater than Version 1.5.0 then you are good to go.

If you see the `command not found` message, you need to install RubyGems or add the executable to your `PATH` variable.

If you see anything less than Version 1.5.0, update the version by running the following command:

```
gem update --system
```

Installing gems with Bundler

Although you can install and use Capybara quite happily without using **Bundler,** it is worth covering this because Bundler is becoming ubiquitous within the Ruby ecosystem and it is very likely that you will want to use it to manage your project's dependencies.

Bundler is itself a Ruby gem and applies a layer of finer grained dependency management on top of RubyGems. With RubyGems you can only ever have one version of a gem installed on your system; with Bundler you can isolate dependencies to a specific project.

Run the following command to install Bundler:

```
gem install bundler
```

In your project directory, create a file named `Gemfile` with the following contents:

```
source 'https://rubygems.org'

gem 'capybara'
```

Then at a command prompt within that directory run:

```
bundle install
```

This will install and link the gems you specified in your `Gemfile` (as well as all their dependencies) with your current project. This will prevent you from accidentally breaking another project that might, for example, depend on an earlier version of the **Nokogiri** gem and will generally make your life a lot easier.

Bundler allows you to declare specific version requirements in your project `Gemfile` and provides many other options such as retrieving a gem directly from a GitHub repository. You can also bundle gems to a local directory under your project. See `http://gembundler.com` for more details of this awesome gem.

Installing system libraries

On some platforms certain gems have a dependency on system libraries. This is usually done for performance reasons. Ruby is an interpreted language so tasks, such as parsing XML can be slow; therefore, it makes sense to delegate that task to a system library.

On Windows you won't need to worry about this, though you will have to ensure you have the Ruby DevKit installed; see `http://rubyinstaller.org/add-ons/devkit` for detailed instructions on how to do this.

Capybara has a dependency on Nokogiri, the popular Ruby-based XML parser. This in turn needs the following system libraries to be available:

- `libxml2`
- `libxml2-dev`
- `libxslt`
- `libxslt-dev`

> The latest version of Nokogiri now includes these dependencies within the gem itself. It is still worth installing the system libraries globally, however, as you will surely encounter projects that rely on versions of Nokogiri prior to 1.6.0.

How you install these on a particular system will differ, for example, `apt-get` for Ubuntu, `yum` for Red Hat, or `brew` for Mac OS X.

Installing Capybara

Your system is now ready for a painless installation of Capybara. How you install the gem will depend on whether you choose to use RubyGems directly or Bundler within your project.

Using RubyGems

If you decide to go without Bundler, installing Capybara is as simple as:

```
gem install capybara
```

If all goes well, you should see an output like the following at your command prompt. The precise output might differ slightly depending on how many of the dependencies you already had installed:

```
Fetching: mime-types-1.25.gem (100%)
Fetching: rack-1.5.2.gem (100%)
Fetching: rack-test-0.6.2.gem (100%)
Fetching: xpath-2.0.0.gem (100%)
Fetching: capybara-2.1.0.gem (100%)
IMPORTANT! Some of the defaults have changed in Capybara 2.1. If you're
experiencing failures,
please revert to the old behaviour by setting:

    Capybara.configure do |config|
      config.match = :one
      config.exact_options = true
      config.ignore_hidden_elements = true
      config.visible_text_only = true
    end

If you're migrating from Capybara 1.x, try:

    Capybara.configure do |config|
      config.match = :prefer_exact
      config.ignore_hidden_elements = false
    end

Details here: http://www.elabs.se/blog/60-introducing-capybara-2-1

Successfully installed mini_portile-0.5.1
Successfully installed nokogiri-1.6.0
```

```
Successfully installed mime-types-1.25
Successfully installed rack-1.5.2
Successfully installed rack-test-0.6.2
Successfully installed xpath-2.0.0
Successfully installed capybara-2.1.0
7 gems installed
```

Using Bundler

If you are using Bundler, ensure you have a file named `Gemfile` in the root directory of your project directory and it contains the following:

```
source 'https://rubygems.org'

gem 'capybara'
```

Then install the necessary gems by running the following command:

```
bundle install
```

If everything is successful, you should see an output like the following:

```
$ bundle install
Fetching gem metadata from https://rubygems.org/.........
Installing mime-types (1.25)
Installing mini_portile (0.5.1)
Installing nokogiri (1.6.0)
Installing rack (1.5.2)
Installing rack-test (0.6.2)
Installing xpath (2.0.0)
Installing capybara (2.1.0)
Using bundler (1.3.5)
Your bundle is complete!
```

Installing Cucumber and Selenium

Capybara is simply an API that provides a layer of abstraction on top of your actual automation library. If it helps, think of Capybara as your translator; you tell it to do something and it translates a nice elegant command into the API of your given driver (which can be a lot less friendly).

So to use this translator we need to have both a way of telling it what to do and also an automation library API for it to translate in to.

Capybara is a very flexible library and throughout this book we will see it used in a variety of settings; however, by far the most common use case is to employ Cucumber as the test runner with Capybara driving Selenium WebDriver to carry out the browser automation.

Cucumber allows the execution of behavior-driven development (BDD) scenarios written in the Gherkin syntax to drive your tests. If you are not overly familiar with Cucumber, `http://cukes.info` should be your first port of call but don't worry it's very straightforward and we will walk through creating your first scenario.

Here is an example Cucumber scenario, which we are going to automate:

```
Feature: Search for Videos on YouTube

  Scenario: Search for Videos of Large Rodents
    Given I am on the YouTube home page
    When I search for "capybara"
    Then videos of large rodents are returned
```

When Cucumber is invoked it parses the plain English scenario and using regular expressions it matches each line to an actual line of Ruby code, called a **step definition**. We will use Capybara to implement these steps. Capybara will then handle the communication with Selenium WebDriver, which will open the browser and start automating the scenario.

The following diagram illustrates the flow from Cucumber through to the underlying driver with Capybara sitting in the middle acting as a translator:

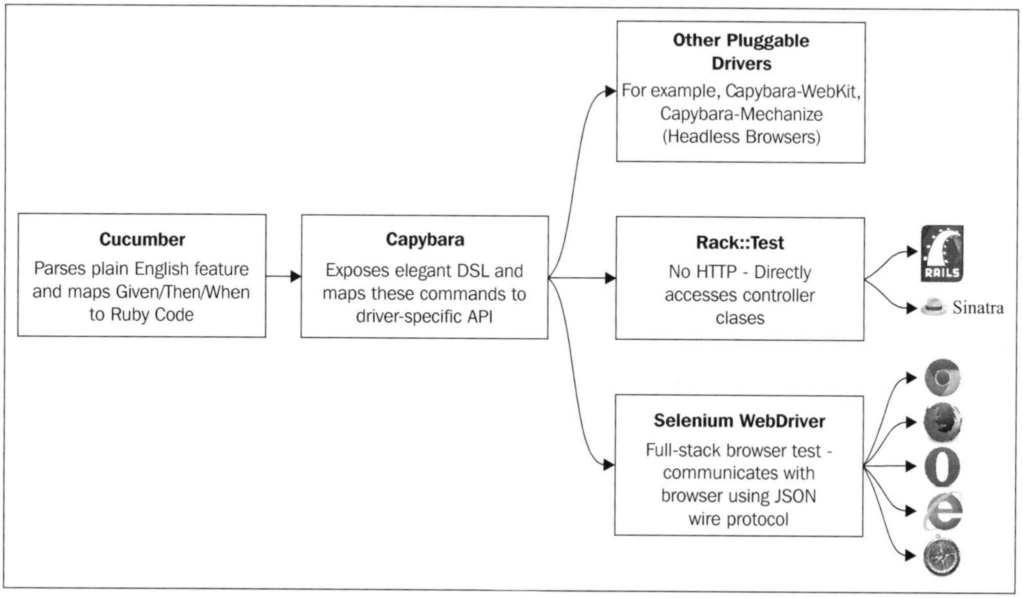

Cucumber and Selenium WebDriver are just additional gems. To install them, run the following:

```
gem install cucumber selenium-webdriver
```

> If you are using Bundler, add `cucumber` and `selenium-webdriver` to your `Gemfile` and run the `bundle install` command again.

In versions of Capybara prior to 2.1, Selenium WebDriver was declared as a runtime dependency in which case it would have been installed when you installed Capybara and a separate installation would not have been required.

Cucumber-Rails

If you are using Capybara to test a Rails application, you should install the Cucumber-Rails gem as opposed to the standard Rails gem.

This gem has both Capybara and Cucumber declared as dependencies, so you will get these for free when you install the gem. To install Cucumber-Rails, simply run the following command:

```
gem install cucumber-rails
```

Alternatively, add this to your `Gemfile` if you are using Bundler, so it looks like the following:

```
source 'https://rubygems.org'

gem 'cucumber-rails'
```

Your first scenario – a YouTube search

Now that we have everything we need, let's get cracking and automate our first scenario, a simple YouTube search:

```
Feature: Search for Videos on YouTube

    Scenario: Search for Videos of Large Rodents
        Given I am on the YouTube home page
        When I search for "capybara"
        Then videos of large rodents are returned
```

A full guide to using Cucumber is outside the scope of this book, but let's assume you have a file/directory set up something like the one shown here, and that you can run features from the command line using Cucumber.

> If you are using Bundler, run Cucumber using the following command:
>
> **`bundle exec cucumber`**
>
> This will ensure you get the Cucumber executable from your project gem bundle and not any global gems.

```
features/
├── youtube_search.feature
├── step_defs
│   └── steps.rb
└── support
    └── env.rb
```

Assuming you have a feature file containing the scenario text, when you run Cucumber from the command line you should get the step definition stubs generated:

```
$ bundle exec cucumber
Feature: Search for Videos on YouTube


  Scenario: Search for Videos of Large Rodents
    Given I am on the YouTube home page
    When I search for "capybara"
    Then videos of large rodents are returned


1 scenario (1 undefined)
3 steps (3 undefined)
0m0.014s
You can implement step definitions for undefined steps with these
snippets:
Given(/^I am on the YouTube home page$/) do
  pending # express the regexp above with the code you wish you had
end


When(/^I search for "(.*?)"$/) do |arg1|
  pending # express the regexp above with the code you wish you had
end


Then(/^videos of large rodents are returned$/) do
  pending # express the regexp above with the code you wish you had
end
```

Copy and paste the snippets output by Cucumber into your `steps.rb` file. These are the stubs that we will complete with our Capybara commands.

If you run Cucumber again, you will now see it reporting that these steps exist but are not implemented:

```
$ bundle exec cucumber
Feature: Search for Videos on YouTube


  Scenario: Search for Videos of Large Rodents
    Given I am on the YouTube home page
```

```
      TODO (Cucumber::Pending)
    When I search for "capybara"
    Then videos of large rodents are returned

1 scenario (1 pending)
3 steps (2 skipped, 1 pending)
0m0.003s
```

We now have enough code to bring Capybara into the picture. We will start off by adding the minimum amount of code needed to get started with the automation.

Ensure your `env.rb` file looks like the following:

```
require 'capybara/cucumber'

Capybara.default_driver = :selenium
```

We start by adding `require 'capybara/cucumber'`; this is all we need to load the necessary files.

> On older versions of RubyGems you may need to add `require 'rubygems'` to your `env.rb` file and if using Bundler, you will also need to add `require 'bundler/setup'`.

We then need to tell Capybara to use the Selenium driver using:

```
Capybara.default_driver = :selenium
```

It is important to reiterate again that Capybara is simply acting as a translator and allows us to talk to any compatible driver. In this instance we use Selenium WebDriver because it is the most popular open source browser automation tool and allows us to test in a real browser, which is useful for our first ever web test.

If you don't set the driver, you may see an error like the following:

```
$ bin/cucumber
Feature: Search for Videos on YouTube

  Scenario: Search for Videos of Large Rodents
    Given I am on the YouTube home page
      rack-test requires a rack application, but none was given
      (ArgumentError)
    When I search for "capybara"
```

```
    Then videos of large rodents are returned


Failing Scenarios:
cucumber features/youtube_search.feature:3 # Scenario: Search for Videos
of Large Rodents


1 scenario (1 failed)
3 steps (1 failed, 2 skipped)
0m0.178s
```

By default, Capybara assumes that you wish to test a Rack application. Rack is an ingenious piece of middleware used in both the Rails and Sinatra frameworks that allows full-stack testing of client/server interaction without the overhead of HTTP, thus making tests very fast. We will cover this in depth later in the book when we discuss how Capybara can be used to test Rails and Sinatra applications.

All that remains now is to fill in the step definitions with our Ruby code that will call the Capybara API to drive the test.

Ensure your `steps.rb` file looks like the following:

```
Given(/^I am on the YouTube home page$/) do
  visit 'http://www.youtube.com'
end

When(/^I search for "(.*?)"$/) do |search_term|
  fill_in 'search_query', :with => search_term
  click_on 'search-btn'
end

Then(/^videos of large rodents are returned$/) do
  page.should have_content 'Largest Rodent'
end
```

Before we dissect the code, let's run the test and see what happens. As always, run your test using the command `cucumber`.

Hopefully you see Firefox open, navigate to the YouTube home page and then search YouTube for videos of Capybara.

Congratulations! You have just successfully run your first full-stack test using Capybara.

> The only issue I can see you might have here is if you don't have Firefox installed or you have it installed to a custom location and Selenium can't find the executable.

Let's briefly look at each step before we dive deep into Capybara's rich API. Here you will see how elegant Capybara's API is, as the code literally needs no explanation. Hopefully this demonstrates that when twinned with Cucumber we have a human-readable specification, which is automated by code that is very expressive. For anybody who has lived through using some of the commercially available test automation tools this should be a revelation!

The first line tells Capybara to inform the driver (Selenium WebDriver) to open a browser and navigate to a URL we provide as a string:

```
visit 'http://www.youtube.com'
```

> Selenium WebDriver has built-in mechanisms to wait for page loads in the browser so we don't have to worry about any kind of page load check. Note that this does not include waiting for asynchronous JavaScript, for example, Ajax/XHTTP requests. Fortunately Capybara has this covered, as we will discover in due course.

After this we need to enter our search terms and click on the **Search** button. So we tell Capybara to get the driver to fill in the search form with our search terms. Again Capybara's API is helpful in telling us this.

```
#note the search_term variable is passed from the Cucumber scenario
fill_in 'search_query', :with => search_term
click_on 'search-btn'
```

The only source of confusion here might be the use of the string literal `search_query` in the `fill_in` method. A lot of Capybara's methods use a "best guess" strategy when you tell them to find something on the page. That is to say they look at various attributes on DOM elements to try to find the one you asked for. In this instance, we know the `name` attribute on the YouTube search form element is `search_query` so this is what we provided.

Finally we need to check if the results returned by the search were relevant. For this, we use Capybara's built-in RSpec magic matchers. If you don't know much about RSpec, there is plenty online (`http://rspec.info/`) but essentially the matchers provide semantically friendly ways of asserting the state of something is as you expect, with the difference to traditional assertions being that they raise exceptions when conditions are not met (as opposed to returning false).

```
page.should have_content 'Largest Rodent'
```

Finally it is worth noting that the `have_content` matcher has a default wait built into it. This is useful because if the content we are waiting for happens to be loaded via asynchronous JavaScript (and not part of the initial page load), Capybara will retry for a configurable amount of time to see if it exists. We will cover strategies for handling asynchronous JavaScript in depth later.

> **Downloading the example code**
>
> You can download the example code files for all Packt books you have purchased from your account at `http://www.PacktPub.com`. If you purchased this book elsewhere, you can visit `http://www.PacktPub.com/support` and register to have the files e-mailed directly to you.

Summary

The aim of this chapter was to get you to a point where you have automated your first scenario using Capybara. We checked if you had Ruby and RubyGems available and installed Capybara and its dependencies as well as Cucumber as our test runner. Finally we implemented a simple scenario that automated a YouTube search; hopefully this has given you a glimpse of Capybara's elegant API, which we will be investigating in more detail in the next chapter.

2

Mastering the API

The YouTube search example showed how easy it was to automate scenarios using Capybara. Now we need to tackle the API head on, focusing on the following topics:

- Selectors – XPath or CSS?
- Navigating
- Submitting forms
- Finders, scoping, and multiple matches
- Asserting and querying

By the end of this chapter, you should feel comfortable automating your own applications using Capybara.

Locating elements with XPath and CSS

The Document Object Model (DOM) is a tree-like "in memory" structure, which browsers construct when parsing an HTML page and processing JavaScript that exists either inline in the page or loaded via `script` tags. CSS selectors and XPath queries allow us to search this structure to find content and Capybara is wholly reliant on such selectors to be able to locate content within web pages. It is therefore essential we understand these before moving into the API.

> Don't let anybody try to tell you XPath is faster than CSS or vice versa. Capybara, in fact, translates all CSS selectors to XPath so we can close the lid firmly on that can of worms!

Here are some simple examples of each type of selector. For example, finding an element whose `id` attribute has the value `'main'`:

- XPath: `//*[@id='main']`
- CSS: `#main`

Finding a direct or indirect child of any `<div>` element with the class `'container'`:

- XPath: `//div//*[@class='container']`
- CSS: `div .container`

The most important thing to consider when implementing a selector is to use the least fragile one possible to retrieve the element you want. For example, the following would be an example of a very bad XPath expression:

```
/html/body/div/div/div/div/p[1]
```

Any change in the structure of the page is likely to break this selector as it relies on the DOM hierarchy not changing, which is not a reasonable expectation in any application under development.

It is much better to get to an element via the most direct route. Often that means using a combination of the type of element and an attribute value, for example, `id`, `class`, or `name`.

> Web applications designed to be accessible will greatly help you because often they use standards, such as **WAI-ARIA** (`http://www.w3.org/WAI/intro/aria`) to add semantic, meaningful, and consistent attributes to elements.

The type of selector you choose is entirely up to you, though I would endeavor to be consistent within your tests to aid understanding.

I am going to use CSS selectors throughout this book as I find them a bit more readable than XPath.

Default selector in Capybara

Capybara uses CSS as the default selector. This means when you use the API you will not need to specify what selector to use, as in the following example:

```
page.find('#maincontent')
```

If you wish to use XPath selectors, you have a couple of choices. Firstly, you can explicitly state this when calling methods:

```
page.find(:xpath, //*[@id="maincontent"])
```

Alternatively, you can set it globally. This code should probably go in your `env.rb` file if you are using Cucumber, as in the following example:

```
require 'capybara/cucumber'

Capybara.default_selector = :xpath
Capybara.default_driver = :selenium
```

> Capybara supports CSS3 selectors, so for all you power users, feel free to get going with `:nth-child`, `:nth-of-type`, and all the other treats CSS3 has in store.

A helping hand with selectors

There are a couple of really useful things that will help you if you are not confident with either XPath or CSS selectors.

The first option is that in both recent Firefox and Chrome browsers if you navigate to a JavaScript console, using either Firebug in Firefox or the Developer Tools in Chrome, you can try out your CSS selectors and play around till you find the best one for the job. To do this you just use a CSS selector with a double dollar (`$$`) before it as in the following screenshot, which shows a Firebug console in Firefox. The same applies to the Developer Tools in Chrome.

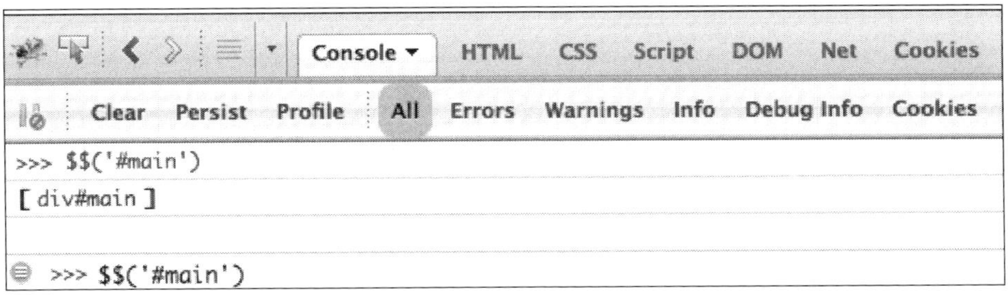

The second option is to install a browser extension, which is definitely worth doing if you plan to use XPath as your default selector.

I have found the Firefox add-on **FirePath** (`https://addons.mozilla.org/en-us/firefox/addon/firepath/`) to be very good for this purpose allowing you to enter XPath or CSS selectors and then highlight matched elements in the DOM.

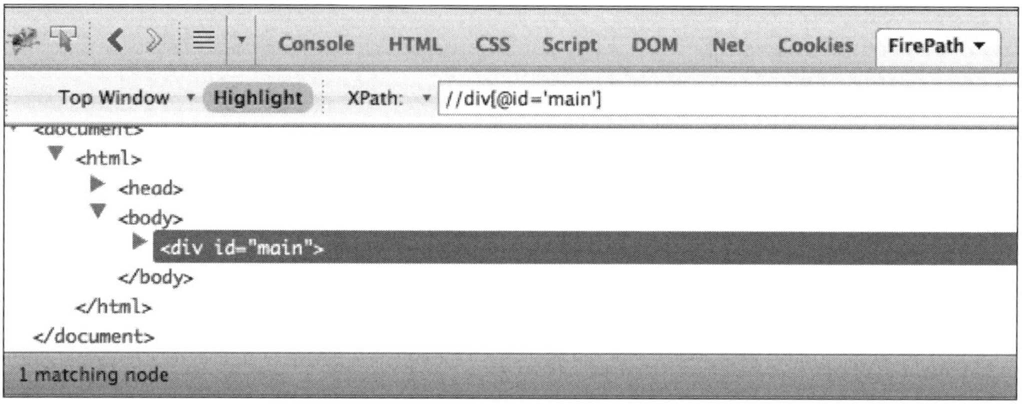

Navigation

The first parts of the Capybara API you will need to get familiar with are the methods available for navigating around your application.

We have already used one such method in our YouTube search scenario:

```
Given(/^I am on the YouTube home page$/) do
  visit 'http://www.youtube.com'
end
```

As you would expect, this code results in Capybara opening the browser if necessary and navigating to the URL provided.

Clicking on links or buttons

There are a few methods we can use to navigate the application using links or buttons:

- `click_link_or_button`
- `click_on`
- `click_link`

Here are some examples of how we could use these. The markup provided is just a snippet from a web page so you can see how the API is used in context:

```
<div id="main">
    <div class="section">
        <a id="myanchor" title="myanchortitle" href="#">Click this
           Anchor</a>
     </div>
</div>
```

Any of the following Cucumber steps would successfully click on the link:

```
When(/^I click on a link using an id$/) do
  click_on 'myanchor'
end

When(/^I click on a link using text$/) do
  click_link_or_button 'Click this Anchor'
end

When(/^I click on a link using the title attribute$/) do
  click_link 'myanchortitle'
end
```

In these examples, we have used a mixture of the three different API methods available and we have also used different selectors each time.

We saw in the "YouTube search" example that Capybara often uses a "best guess" strategy for much of the API when attempting to locate elements. In the case of links and buttons, Capybara looks at the following element properties when attempting to locate the element to click on:

- The `id` attribute of the `anchor`, `button`, or `input` tag
- The `title` attribute of the `anchor`, `button`, or `input` tag
- Text within the `anchor`, `button`, or `input` tag
- The `value` attribute of the `input` element where its type is one of `'button'`, `'reset'`, `'submit'`, or `'image'`
- The `alt` attribute where an image is used as an anchor or input

We can apply the same methods against the following markup to click on a button element:

```
<div id="main">
  <div class="section">
    <button id="mybutton" title="mybuttontitle">Click this
                Button</button>
  </div>
</div>


When(/^I click on a button using an id$/) do
  click_on 'mybutton'
end
```

The same is true when the markup contains an `input` element of `type="button"`.

Submitting forms

Another common task you are likely to want to automate is the completion and submission of forms.

Again Capybara provides a lot of user-friendly API to do just this. Consider this simple form snippet:

```
<form id="myform">
    <input type="text" name="Forename" value="" />
    <input type="text" name="Surname" value="" />
    <input type="submit" value="Go" />
</form>
```

The following Cucumber step definition would fill in and submit the form:

```
When(/^I complete and submit the form$/) do
  fill_in 'Forename', :with => 'Matthew'
  fill_in 'Surname', :with => 'Robbins'
  click_on 'Go'
end
```

When locating fields that can accept text input, Capybara will use one of the following to find those fields in the DOM:

- The `id` attribute of the `input` element
- The `name` attribute of the `input` element
- A related `label` element

An example using `label` elements is shown in the following code. Labels are more commonly associated with radio buttons and checkboxes but they can still be used with text inputs:

```
<form id="myform">
   <label for="name1">User Forename</label>
   <input id="name1" type="text" name="Forename" value="" />
   <label for="name2">User Surname</label>
   <input id="name2" type="text" name="Surname" value="" />
   <input type="submit" value="Go" />
</form>

When(/^I complete and submit the form$/) do
  fill_in 'User Forename', :with => 'Matthew'
  fill_in 'User Surname', :with => 'Robbins'
  click_on 'Go'
end
```

Checkboxes and radio buttons

You are also likely to encounter forms that have checkboxes and radio buttons on them. Thankfully, the API to manipulate these elements is much the same as completing text inputs.

The following markup now includes some additional elements and a screenshot is shown so that you can visualize what this would look like when rendered in a browser:

```
<form id="myform">
    <label for="name1">User Forename</label>
    <input id="name1" type="text" name="Forename" value="" />
    <label for="name2">User Surname</label>
    <input id="name2" type="text" name="Surname" value="" />
    <p>
      <label for="title">Title</label>
      <select name="user_title" id="title">
        <option>Mrs</option>
        <option>Mr</option>
        <option>Miss</option>
      </select>
    </p>
    <p>
      <label for="under_16">Under 16</label>
      <input type="radio" name="underage" value="under"
               id="under_16" checked="checked"/>
```

```
        <label for="over_16">Over 16</label>
        <input type="radio" name="overage" value="over"
                 id="over_16"/>
      </p>
      <p>
        <label for="consent">Consent Given?</label>
        <input type="checkbox" value="yes" name="consent_checkbox"
               id="consent"/>
      </p>
      <input type="submit" value="Go" />
</form>
```

This will generate an output as shown in the following screenshot:

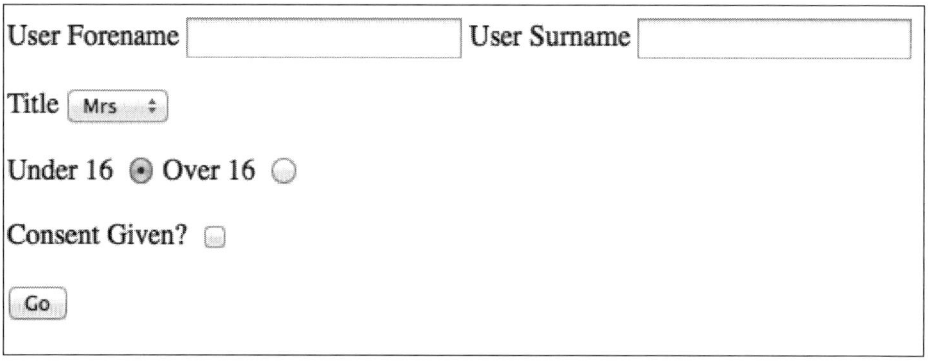

We now need to implement steps to manipulate the form using the drop-down menus, radio buttons, and checkboxes. These are all just `input` elements of type `select`, `radio`, and `checkbox` respectively.

```
When(/^I complete and submit the form$/) do
  fill_in 'User Forename', :with => 'Matthew'
  fill_in 'User Surname', :with => 'Robbins'
  select 'Mr', :from => 'title'
  choose 'Over 16'
  check 'consent'
  click_on 'Go'
end
```

We have already covered filling in the text fields. Next, we move on to selecting the title from the drop-down list:

```
select 'Mr', :from => 'title'
```

As with the `input` elements Capybara will again look at related labels, the `id` and `name` attributes, to locate the element. In this instance `title` is the ID of the `select` element. The value to select from the list must be the text of one of the child `option` elements.

> Capybara also has an `unselect` method, which does exactly what you would expect; it clears the selection!

The next element to tackle is the radio button selection. Here we use the following code:

```
choose 'Over 16'
```

Capybara's `choose` method again looks at related labels, the `id` and `name` attributes, to locate the element. In this instance, `Over 16` is the label related to the radio input with the `id` value as `over_16`.

Finally, we need to select the `Consent` checkbox and for this we use:

```
check 'consent'
```

Capybara's `check` method, as with the others, uses related labels, the `id` and `name` attributes to locate the element. In this instance `consent` is the `id` value related to the checkbox input.

> Capybara also has an `uncheck` method, which does exactly what you would expect; it clears the checkbox!

Finally, Capybara also provides API to allow you to upload files by setting the path in an `input` element of `type='file'`. Here is an example of markup containing such an element:

```
<label for="form_image">Image</label>
<input type="file" name="image" id="form_image"/>
```

And an example step to implement this would be as follows:

```
When(/^I attach a file in a form$/) do
  attach_file 'Image', '/Users/matt/foo.png'
end
```

Capybara will validate that the file to which you are trying to set the path actually exists on the filesystem. If it does not, you will see an error message like the following:

```
cannot attach file,  /Users/matt/foo.png does not exist
(Capybara::FileNotFound)
      ./features/step_defs/form.rb:11:
```

Finders, scoping, and multiple matches

A lot of the API we have covered so far in this chapter has in some ways been a bit of a façade. Capybara, in the best way possible, provides a lot of "syntactic sugar" around some basic building blocks.

These building blocks are in fact simply XPath expressions to find things on the page and then delegate the action down to the underlying driver.

Most of the time it makes sense to use this "sugared" API, as your code is made a lot more expressive and readable. Aside from the obvious benefit of "write once, run on multiple drivers", the clean semantics of Capybara's API are its main selling points so you should use it wherever possible.

However, there will be times when these methods don't work for you. For example, the `click_on` method is great for handling navigation via anchor tags and images, but what if your site uses a lot of JavaScript to register click events on other elements?

Consider the following (fairly useless) web page:

```
<html>
  <head>
    <title>Click Examples</title>
    <script>
      window.onload = function() {
          var mydiv = document.getElementById("mydiv");

          mydiv.onclick =function() {
              alert('div has been clicked');
          };

      };
    </script>
  </head>
<body>
```

```
    <div id="main">
      <div class="section">
        <div id="mydiv" title="mydivtitle">Click This Div</div>
        </div>
      </div>
    </body>
  </html>
```

In this instance, clicking on the `div` element with the `id` value of `mydiv` results in an alert message.

To automate this click, we need to turn to Capybara's so called "finders". To begin, let's focus our attention on the `find` method itself. This is a method that takes an XPath expression or a CSS selector and returns a `Capybara::Element` on which we can invoke an action.

A Cucumber step to do that would look something like this:

```
When(/^I click on a div with a click handler attached$/) do
  find('#mydiv').click
end
```

Because we chose CSS selectors as the default selector, we don't need to tell Capybara this; however, if we wanted to use an XPath we would simply pass `:xpath` as the first argument to the method and then the XPath expression as the second argument.

Nearly all the other finder methods are built on top of this but are a little more sugared:

- `find_field`: This finder searches for form fields by the related `label` element, or the `name`/`id` attribute
- `field_labeled`: This finder is the same as `find_field`
- `find_link`: This finder finds an anchor or an image link using the `text`, `id`, or `img alt` attribute
- `find_button`: This finder finds a button by the `id`, `name`, or `value` attribute
- `find_by_id`: This finder finds any element by the `id` attribute

As you can see finders are extremely powerful allowing us to locate any element in the DOM and manipulate it.

Multiple matches

So far all the examples we have looked at make the assumption that we are looking for a single element in the DOM. With dynamic web applications you may not know exactly which element to look for. For example, let's assume you are checking some search results that are dynamically added to the page:

```
<div id="main">
  <h1>Search Results</h1>
  <ul class="section">
    <li id="res1" class="result">Match 1</li>
    <li id="res2" class="result">Match 2</li>
    <li id="res3" class="result">Match 3</li>
   </ul>
</div>
```

There are a couple of things you could do here to assert that the content you expect to be returned exists. The most obvious and perhaps the one you might turn to first is to iterate through the results and inspect each one. For this you can use the `all` method, which returns a collection of elements:

```
When(/^I search for the relevant result$/) do
  all('.result').each_with_index do |elem, idx|
    elem.text.should == "Match #{idx + 1}"
  end
end
```

Here we are iterating through all the search results in the preceding markup and checking that the text is what we expect that is, the first element contains `Match 1`, the second `Match 2`, and so on.

There are some alternatives to using the `all` method, which may be more appropriate. If you don't need to check each match, you can set your matching strategy to be more intelligent looking perhaps for partial matches or try passing in some additional arguments to ensure the element is visible and contains specific text. Following the release of Capybara 2.1 there has been significant change in this area so it makes sense to cover this in depth.

Matching strategies

Looking again at the previous search results markup, let's see what happens when you use the `find` method to retrieve elements with the class `result`:

```
When(/^I search for the relevant result$/) do
  find('.result').text
end
```

Running this code produces the following error:

```
When I search for the relevant result          # features/step_defs/
results.rb:5
      Ambiguous match, found 3 elements matching css ".result"
         (Capybara::Ambiguous)
```

Capybara is letting you know that there is more than one element matching this query, which makes sense. We don't want Capybara to be too magical and just assume we want the first match; this could be dangerous.

> Capybara 1.0 would just take the first of multiple matches, which could result in your code grabbing the incorrect element and causing you headaches when debugging broken tests.

Capybara 2.1 introduced the `Capybara.match` and `Capybara.exact` options to allow you to fine-tune the strategy employed when attempting to find elements on the page. The possible options for `Capybara.match` are:

- `:one` – This option will raise a `Capybara::Ambiguous` exception when more than one match is found for the query.
- `:first` – This option will simply pick the first match (the old behavior).
- `:prefer_exact` – This option will return an exact matching element, if multiple matches are found, some of which are exact, and others are not.
- `:smart` – This option is available by default in Capybara 2.1 and is dependent on the value of `Capybara.exact`. If this is set to `true`, the behavior is the same as `:one`. Otherwise, Capybara first searches for exact matches, if multiple matches are found, a `Capybara::Ambiguous` exception is raised, if none are found, it searches for inexact matches again raising `Capybara::Ambiguous` if multiple matches are returned.

Here is an example to illustrate the different options. Hopefully you won't have markup like this in your application but it serves to illustrate how the different strategies will affect which elements get returned from a query.

```
<label for="text1">please complete this field</label>
<input id="text1" type="text"/>
<label for="text2">please complete this</label>
<input id="text2" type="text" />
<label for="text3">please complete this input</label>
<input id="text3" type="text" />
```

```
page.fill_in 'please complete this', :with => 'foobar'
page.fill_in 'please complete', :with => 'bazqux'
```

Remember, the default behavior when not using XPath or CSS selectors is that Capybara will try to perform a partial string match. In the preceding example, the first search term `please complete this` is a partial match for the labels `please complete this field` and `please complete this input`. The second search term `please complete` is a partial match for all three labels.

Let's consider each strategy in turn and see how this would affect which input gets completed and with what value:

- `Capybara.match = :one` - This strategy raises the `Capybara::Ambiguous` exception.
- `Capybara.match = :first` - In this strategy, both the `fill_in` calls will fill in the first text input as they are both partial matches for the first label.
- `Capybara.match = :prefer_exact` - In this strategy, the second input will be completed with `foobar` as its label is an exact match for the first query. Capybara will fall back to filling in `bazqux` for the first input as its label is the **first** partial match for the second query. Note this query is also a partial match for the second and third input but with this strategy the first of any multiple matches is used.
- `Capybara.match = :smart` - In this strategy, the second input will be completed with `foobar` its label is an exact match for the first query. However, unlike with `:prefer_exact` a `Capybara::Ambiguous`, an error is raised for the second `fill_in` call because there is more than one partial match.

> Note if you set `Capybara.exact = :true`, this will override the previous strategies and no partial matches will be considered. Instead the `Capybara::ElementNotFound` exception will be raised if a query only partially matches elements on the page.

The behavior of `:smart` also extends to choosing options from a drop-down list (the `select` element).

As you can see, these strategies are quite hard to get to grips with, so I would recommend you create some of your own test pages and then play around with the different options until you are comfortable with what is going to work best in your production tests.

Element visibility

The visibility of an element also affects whether Capybara will locate it in the DOM. Capybara has a global setting, which it uses to determine whether to check for hidden elements:

```
Capybara.ignore_hidden_elements = true
```

The default value for this setting is now `true`, which means that the elements that are not visible to the user (for example, they have CSS properties set such as `display: none` or `visibility: hidden`) will not get returned as results from our queries.

The behavior of the `text` method has also changed somewhat in Capybara 2.1. This is typically used as follows:

```
find('#log').text #finds text within the element with the id 'log'
```

The behavior of this method is now dependent on the value of `Capybara.ignore_hidden_elements`. When this is true only visible text is returned, otherwise all text is returned.

> In Capybara 1.0 the behavior of this method was driver dependent; Selenium WebDriver only returned visible text but Rack::Test would return anything. In Capybara 2.0 consistency was enforced and both drivers only ever returned visible text.

Capybara 2.1 also introduced a method to override the behavior of `Capybara.ignore_hidden_elements` for the `text` method. If you set `Capybara.visible_text_only = true`, the behavior of the `text` method will be to only ever return visible text regardless of whether `ignore_hidden_elements` is set to `false`.

> It is important to remember driver behavior may still differ depending on how sophisticated the driver's interpretation of visibility is. In Rack::Test this will be quite crude as there is no rendering as opposed to Selenium where pages are fully rendered. Hence, the browser can apply a more sophisticated interpretation of whether an element is visible to the user.

Finally it is worth noting that you can set all these options in a configure block. For example:

```
Capybara.configure do |config|
  config.match = :smart
  config.exact_options = true
end
```

Scoping

When attempting to find content on the page that might not be easy to uniquely identify, another option is to restrict the query to a section of the page. Capybara provides the `within` method to allow scoped queries:

```
<div id="main">
  <h1>Search Results</h1>
  <ul id="local_results">
    <li id="res1" class="result">Local Match 1</li>
    <li id="res2" class="result">Local Match 2</li>
    <li id="res3" class="result">Local Match 3</li>
  </ul>
  <ul id="internet_results">
    <li id="res4" class="result">Internet Match 1</li>
    <li id="res5" class="result">Internet Match 2</li>
    <li id="res6" class="result">Internet Match 3</li>
  </ul>
</div>
```

In the preceding example, we have two sets of search results returned, some from the local site and some from the Internet. Let's assume we want to find all the results from the Internet.

```
When(/^I search for results within a scope$/) do
  within('#internet_results') do
    all('.result').each do |elem|
      puts elem.text
    end
  end
end
```

Running this step would produce the following output:

```
Internet Match 1
Internet Match 2
Internet Match 3
```

The argument to the `within` method is just the same as with `find`. If no type is provided, the single argument is assumed to be a selector of the default type. Capybara also provides some `within` methods that scope to a specific type of element:

- `within_fieldset` – The first argument should be the `id` or `legend` attribute within a form `fieldset` element
- `within_table` – The first argument should be the `id` or `caption` attribute within a `table` element

- `within_frame(frame_id)` - The first argument should be the `id` value of an `iframe` element (selected drivers, for example, Selenium)
- `within_window` - The first argument should be the `window` handle (selected drivers for example, Selenium)

Asserting and querying

Now that you can navigate around your application, submit forms, and locate any element in the DOM, we need to turn our attention to validating the expected behavior.

Capybara allows us to do this in a couple of ways.

The first option is to use the Capybara "Query" API directly. Capybara provides a whole set of methods for querying the page under test and returning a Boolean value.

```
page.has_content? 'capybara rocks'
page.has_selector? '#main'
```

You could use these methods with a traditional "assertion" approach where tests assert against a Boolean condition. The other option is to use RSpec "Magic Matchers". These matchers in fact just "piggy back" off the query methods:

```
page.should have_content 'capybara rocks'
page.should have_selector '#main'
```

The beauty of using the RSpec matchers is two fold:

- You get meaningful exceptions that inform you exactly where the problem lies
- It satisfies the "fail fast" ideology whereby we fail as early and as hard as possible, which is exactly what we want when testing web apps

Matchers and RSpec

Capybara exposes the following methods for querying your application's pages:

```
has_selector?(*args)
has_no_selector?(*args)
has_xpath?(path, options={})
has_no_xpath?(path, options={})
has_css?(path, options={})
has_no_css?(path, options={})
has_text?(content)
has_content?(content)
```

```
has_no_text?(content)
has_no_content?(content)
has_link?(locator, options={})
has_no_link?(locator, options={})
has_button?(locator)
has_no_button?(locator)
has_field?(locator, options={})
has_no_field?(locator, options={})
has_checked_field?(locator)
has_no_checked_field?(locator)
has_unchecked_field?(locator)
has_no_unchecked_field?(locator)
has_select?(locator, options={})
has_no_select?(locator, options={})
has_table?(locator, options={})
has_no_table?(locator, options={})
```

All of these can be used in isolation or can be wrapped using an RSpec Matcher.

We won't go into too much detail on these query methods because the principles are exactly the same as when using the "finder" methods; the only difference is that rather than returning an element they just return true or false, depending on whether the element or content exists.

Let's return to our "search results" example:

```
<div id="main">
  <h1>Search Results</h1>
  <ul id="local_results">
    <li id="res1" class="result">Local Match 1</li>
    <li id="res2" class="result">Local Match 2</li>
    <li id="res3" class="result">Local Match 3</li>
  </ul>
  <ul id="internet_results">
    <li id="res4" class="result">Internet Match 1</li>
    <li id="res5" class="result">Internet Match 2</li>
    <li id="res6" class="result">Internet Match 3</li>
  </ul>
</div>
```

Here are some example queries and their RSpec equivalents, firstly checking for the existence of a selector, and then checking for text content:

```
Then(/^the desired search results are returned$/) do
  page.has_selector? '#local_results'
  page.should have_selector '#local_results'
```

```
end
Then(/^the desired search results are returned$/) do
  page.should have_content 'Local Match 1'
  first('#res1').should have_content 'Local Match 1'
end
```

Note that these query methods can be used at the page level or on any node retrieved using a finder method.

> If you see the exception `undefined method should for #<Capybara::Session> (NoMethodError)`, you probably need to add `gem install rspec` or add `gem 'rspec'` to your `Gemfile` and run `bundle install` again. You would also need to add `require 'rspec/expectations'` in your `env.rb` file.

As well as checking that elements and content exist we can of course check that things are not present or visible on the page. In the following example, we will check if an element with the `id` value `local_results` does not exist on the page:

```
Then(/^the desired search results are returned$/) do
  page.has_no_selector? '#local_results'
  page.should have_no_selector '#local_results'
end
```

The `has_xpath?`, `has_no_xpath?`, `has_css?`, and `has_no_css?` methods are precisely the same as the `has_selector?` and `has_no_selector?` methods, the only difference being they just specifically take XPath or CSS selectors as arguments.

The methods that look at specific elements such as tables, fields, and links behave exactly like the finder methods we saw earlier where they accept a `locator` argument and then look at different attributes or labels to find those elements.

- `has_link?` - This checks for an anchor or an image link using the `text`, `id`, or `img alt` attribute
- `has_button?` - This checks for a button by the `id`, `name`, or `value` attribute
- `has_field?` - This checks for the associated `label`, `name`, or `id` attribute of a field
- `has_select?` - This checks for the associated `label`, `name`, or `id` attribute of an input of type `select`
- `has_table?` - This checks for the `id` or `caption` element within a `table` element

> It is important to remember that all these methods can be called on any `Capybara::Node` element, meaning you can perform a query on a node that has been returned from the result of a previous query.

Refining finders and matchers

In addition to setting Capybara's configuration globally using options such as `Capybara.match = :smart` you can override the behavior on single finder or matcher statements by passing an additional hash of arguments, such as `:text`, `:visible`, `:exact`, `:match`, or `:wait`.

Consider this page snippet, which makes some text visible after a delay of five seconds:

```
<head>
  <script>
    $(document).ready(function() {
        var addText = function() {
            $('.section').attr('style', 'visibility;visible;');
        }
        setTimeout(addText, 5000);
    });
  </script>
</head>
<body>
  <div id="main">
    <div class="section" style="visibility:hidden;">Capybara
        Rocks</div>
  </div>
</body>
```

If we have not modified `Capybara.default_timeout`, it won't help here as it defaults to wait for two seconds for asynchronous JavaScript. We can override this, and while we're at it, make our finder check for the correct text as well as override the matching strategy and ensure the text is visible!

```
find('.section', :visible => true, :wait => 10, :text => 'Capybara R',
:match => :first)
```

It's worth stating again that this will override any default settings we may have. This technique can also be used with the `query` methods (such as `page.has_content?`) and also with the `all` method.

For example, let's assume a page has run some JavaScript that has set one of the search results not to be shown:

```
<div id="main">
  <h1>Search Results</h1>
  <ul class="section">
    <li id="res1" class="result">Match 1</li>
    <li id="res2" class="result">Match 2</li>
    <li id="res3" class="result">Match 3</li>
    <li id="res4" class="result" style="visibility:hidden;">Match
      4</li>
    <li id="res5" class="result">Match 5</li>
  </ul>
</div>
```

If we now run the following step:

```
When(/^I search for visible results$/) do
  all('.result', :visible => true).each do |elem|
    puts elem.text
  end
end
```

The output would be:

```
Match 1
Match 2
Match 3
Match 5
```

You can also get the `all` method to return only elements with specific text, for example, if we modified the step again:

```
When(/^I search for the relevant result$/) do
  all('.result', :text => 'Match 1').each do |elem |
    puts elem.text
  end
end
```

Then the output would be:

```
Match 1
```

Checking attribute values

Quite often you will want to check if an element exists and has an attribute with a specific value. This is simple using either CSS selectors or XPath expressions. This example checks for the presence of a `div` element with an `id` attribute of `local_results`:

```
Then(/^the desired search results are returned$/) do
  #using CSS selector
  page.has_selector? 'div[id=local_resuls]'
  #using XPath
  page.has_xpath? "//div[@id='local_results']"
end
```

You can also use an array index notation on any `Capybara::Element` passing in the attribute name as a symbol as shown in the following example. Here we have combined this technique with one of RSpec's default matchers to assert the expected result.

```
Then(/^the desired search results are returned$/) do
  first('#res1')[:class].should == 'result'
end
```

Summary

In this chapter, we have had a guided tour of Capybara's API covering navigation, form filling, finding elements, and validating their content. The good news is that the hard part is now out of the way and you now have all the skills you need to automate your tests with Capybara. In the next chapter, we see how powerful Capybara is for testing Rails and Sinatra apps and begin to uncover the real benefits of using this wonderful library.

3

Testing Rails and Sinatra Applications

Capybara was born out of the ecosystem of tools that exist to support testing Rails applications. We have seen that any web application can be tested using Capybara; however, we should take the time to understand why Capybara is particularly well-suited for testing Rails apps, Sinatra apps, or in fact any Rack application.

In this chapter we will consider the following topics:

- Defining Rack
- Capybara and Rack::Test
- Which driver to use and when
- Capybara, Rails, and transactional fixtures

Understanding the Rack interface

If you hang around long enough on any Ruby message board, IRC (Internet Relay Chat) channel, or Issue Tracker, you will soon hear mention of the mysterious Rack application; so just what is Rack?

Rack (`http://rack.github.io/`) is probably one of the most powerful libraries within the Ruby web application stack and underpins nearly all Ruby-based web frameworks and web servers. Rack is an abstraction layer, often referred to as middleware, sitting between any web application that wants to talk over HTTP and the web server chosen to implement that communication.

What does this mean in practice? Let's say you are implementing a web application framework. At some point you will have to consider how you are going to interface to the web server so that you can digest a request and send a response. Typically, this would have to be done by writing to a bespoke adapter for the given web server. So if you wanted your web framework to run in multiple servers, you would have to code multiple adapters. Rack removes the need for this; you simply code your framework to Rack's very straightforward interface, and Rack handles the communication with the server, so swapping servers is a one-line change!

The following is probably the simplest working example of a Rack application. Try it yourself and you will see there is no magic here, just a very simple but ingenious idea.

> You will need the Rack gem for this. You should have it in your current project as it as a dependency of Capybara; but if you have any issues, be sure to run `gem install rack` or add `gem 'rack'` to your `Gemfile` and run `bundle install`.

```
require 'rack'
require 'rack/server'

class HelloWorld
  def response
    [200, {'Content-Length' => '11'}, ['Hello World']]
  end
end

class HelloWorldApp
  def self.call(env)
    HelloWorld.new.response
  end
end

Rack::Server.start :app => HelloWorldApp
```

This example implements the core Rack method `call` and then responds with a simple `200 OK` status and the body text `Hello World`. Note that rather than using `Rack::Server`, which uses the default WEBrick server, we could have used any Rack-compatible web server here. Swapping this for another server such as Thin (`http://code.macournoyer.com/thin/`) would be as simple as changing the last line to read `Rack::Handler::Thin.start`.

You can start the application by typing `ruby myapp.rb` at the command line; you should then see the following displayed:

```
$ ruby myapp.rb
[2013-04-09 08:29:27] INFO  WEBrick 1.3.1
[2013-04-09 08:29:27] INFO  ruby 1.9.3 (2012-11-10) [x86_64-darwin11.4.2]
[2013-04-09 08:29:27] INFO  WEBrick::HTTPServer#start: pid=32991
port=8080
```

If you navigate to `http://localhost:8080`, you should see the `Hello World` text in the browser, hey presto your own Rack application!

The benefits extend further than just this abstraction, because the communication between the web framework and the web server is done via Rack's specified hash format this means stubbing out requests and responses is straightforward. The test library just has to conform to the hash format for requests and response handling, and you can instantly exercise the application's full-stack functionality without the need for a web server and HTTP. The Rack::Test library provides this functionality and is one of the built-in drivers shipped with Capybara. It is likely to be your first port of call when testing a Rails or Sinatra application with Capybara.

Capybara and Rack::Test

Rack::Test is a library that implements the Rack protocol, making it possible to test your application's full-stack functionality without the latency of HTTP communication and opening real browsers. You can use its API to send a request to your application; when your application responds, Rack::Test will digest the response and allow you to interrogate it. It can do this because it is simply implementing the Rack protocol, constructing the request hash to present to the application just as the Rack web server would do, interpreting the response hash, and making it available to you via the API.

Here is an example using Rack::Test outside of Capybara that tests the "Hello World" application we developed previously:

```
require 'rack/test'
require 'test/unit'

class HelloWorldAppTest < Test::Unit::TestCase
  include Rack::Test::Methods

  def app
```

```
    HelloWorldApp
  end

  def test_redirect_logged_in_users_to_dashboard
    get "/"

    assert last_response.ok?
    assert_equal last_response.body, 'Hello World'
  end

end
```

This test calls our application's home page route, asserts that a 200 HTTP response code was received, and then ensures the body text was `Hello World`. But the crucial thing to remember is that no actual communication over the wire occurred here, so you are getting the reliability and speed of a unit test with the benefit of exercising the application's full stack.

Of course, realistically our application under test is likely to be implemented using frameworks such as Rails or Sinatra; we also want to use Capybara to drive Rack::Test, so we don't have to worry about the internals of Rack::Test.

Rack::Test does not have a direct API for clicking elements, setting radio buttons, dealing with forms, and so on. It is focused more or less solely on performing the Rack transactions for us, effectively stubbing out the web server. Capybara, therefore, has to manage the translation of user-initiated events into Rack::Test actions. As an example, here is how the Capybara driver translates the click event on an element into the relevant method's calls for Rack::Test:

```
def click
    if tag_name == 'a'
      method = self["data-method"] if driver.options[:respect_data_
                method]
      method ||= :get
      driver.follow(method, self[:href].to_s)
    elsif (tag_name == 'input' and %w(submit image).include?(type)) or
        ((tag_name == 'button') and type.nil? or type == "submit")
      Capybara::RackTest::Form.new(driver, form).submit(self)
    end
end
```

Capybara determines the type of element being clicked and then works out whether to tell Rack::Test to follow a link or to submit a form.

Testing a Sinatra application

All of this becomes more tangible if we look at a more realistic example. We will use Sinatra simply because there is less boilerplate code than Rails, but the principles are exactly the same.

Consider the following simple Sinatra application; it allows us to complete a book review and return the data submitted. Note that there is no persistence in this example.

Sinatra application file – app.rb

This is the main file for our Sinatra application that handles the controller logic:

```
require 'sinatra'

class BookReview < Sinatra::Base

  get '/form' do
    erb :form
  end

  post '/submit' do
    @name = params[:name]
    @title = params[:title]
    @review = params[:review]
    @age = params[:age]
    erb :result
  end

end

BookReview.run! if __FILE__ == $0 #only run if invoked from command
line - otherwise leave to Capybara
```

Form template – form.erb

This is an ERB template (Ruby's standard HTML templating format), which when rendered will allow a user to submit a book review:

```
<link rel="stylesheet" href="css/form.css">
<form action="/submit" method="post">
  <header id="header" class="info">
    <h2>Book Reviews</h2>
    <div>Review the last book you purchased...</div>
  </header>
```

```
<ul>
  <li>
  <label for="name">
    Your Name
  </label>
  <input type="text" id="name" name="name" maxlegth="255">
  </li>
  <li>
  <label class="desc" for="age">
    Age Range
  </label>
  <div>
    <select id="age" name="age">
      <option value="-" selected="selected">
      </option>
      <option value="<20" >
      Under 20
      </option>
      <option value="20-50" >
      20 -50
      </option>
      <option value="50+" >
      Over 50
      </option>
    </select>
  </div>
  </li>
  <li>
  <label for="book_title">
    Book Title
  </label>
  <input type="text" id="book_title" name="title"
       maxlegth="255">
  </li>
  <li>
  <label for="review">
    Your Review...
  </label>
  <textarea id="review" name="review" rows="10"
       cols="50"></textarea>
  </li>
  <li>
  <input type="submit" value="Submit"/>
  </li>
 </ul>
</form>
```

This is how the form would look when rendered in the browser:

Results template – result.erb

This is another ERB template, which will render the saved review:

```
<div class="saved_review">
<p>You submitted the following on: <%= Time.new.strftime("%Y-%m-%d
%H:%M:%S") %> </p>
  <ul>
    <li>
    <p id="name">Name: <%= @name %></p>
    </li>
    <li>
    <p id="age">Age: <%= @age %></p>
    </li>
    <li>
    <p>Book Title: <%= @title %></p>
    </li>
```

```
      <li>
      <p>Book Review: <%= @review %></p>
      </li>
    </ul>
    <a href="/form">Submit another review...</a>
  </div>
```

This is how the submitted review will appear in the browser:

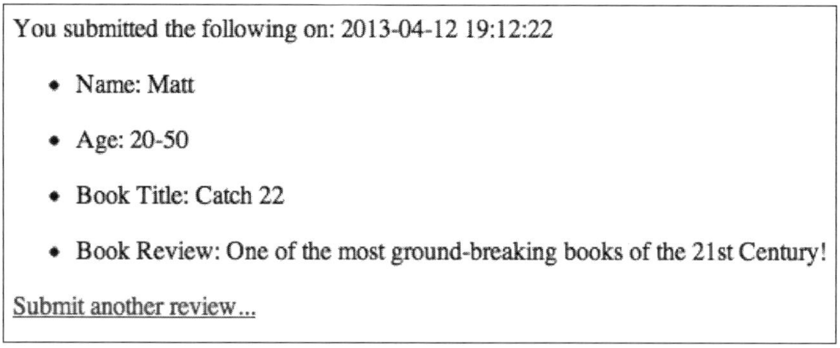

When the application is run from the command line using `ruby app.rb`, you can navigate to `http://localhost:4567/form` and submit a book review; this will then echo back the submitted details at `http://localhost:4567/result`.

So now that we have a working Sinatra application, we need to see how to test this using Capybara and crucially show the difference between testing with Rack::Test as the driver as opposed to Selenium WebDriver.

Testing with Rack::Test

From a Capybara perspective, you interact with your Sinatra/Rails application in exactly the same way in which you do with a remote application. It's just the setup that differs slightly.

For example, here are some Cucumber step definitions with their Capybara implementation to automate the completion of the book review form and check the submitted results:

```
Given(/^I am on a book review site$/) do
  visit('/form')
end

When(/^I submit a book review$/) do
  fill_in 'name', :with => 'Matt'
```

```
  fill_in 'title', :with => 'Catch 22'
  fill_in 'review', :with => 'Alright I guess....'
  select '20 - 50', :from => 'age'
  click_on 'Submit'
end

Then(/^I should see the saved details confirmed$/) do
  page.should have_text 'You submitted the following on:'
  find('#name').should have_text 'Matt'
  find('#age').should have_text '20-50'
  find('#review').should have_text 'Alright I guess....'
  find('#title').should have_text 'Catch 22'
end
```

This implementation is nothing new to us by now, and thankfully this will not change, regardless of the driver we choose, that's the beauty of Capybara.

However, the setup is something we need to look at in a bit more detail. Here is an example `env.rb` file such as you might have in your Cucumber project for testing your Rails or Sinatra application:

```
require 'capybara/cucumber'
require 'rspec/expectations'
require_relative '../../sinatra/app'

Capybara.default_driver = :rack_test

Capybara.register_driver :selenium do |app|
  Capybara::Selenium::Driver.new(app, :browser => :chrome)
end

Capybara.app = BookReview
```

Here we introduce only one new concept, which is setting the value of `Capybara.app` to the `main` class for our Sinatra application, which in this case is the `BookReview` class.

The `Capybara.default_driver` is also set to `:rack_test`, so when we run the tests they will use Rack::Test as opposed to Selenium WebDriver. No browser will open and no HTTP requests made, which means they will run very quickly; yet, as we discussed before, they still exercise the entire application stack.

However, we still want the option of running these tests using Selenium in a real browser. To do this, we simply change the default driver:

```
Capybara.default_dirver = :selenium
```

If you run your tests again, you will notice that as if by magic your application is running in the server and pages are available for the tests to access. If you look closely, you will notice that the application is running on a seemingly random port. Because the application is a Rack app, Capybara is able to start the application server for you and stop it at the end of the tests. In this instance, you are of course exercising your application over HTTP and in a real browser, so tests will clearly run significantly slower.

Just to highlight the speed issues, here are two runs of the same scenario: the first using Rack::Test and the second using Selenium WebDriver. As you can see, the speed difference is significant:

```
$ bin/cucumber -r features features/chapter3/sinatra.feature


Feature: Using Capybara and Rack-Test to Interact with Sinatra App


  Scenario: Complete Book Review                        # features/chapter3/
sinatra.feature:3
    Given I am on a book review site                    # features/chapter3/
steps/sinatra.rb:1
    When I submit a book review                         # features/chapter3/
steps/sinatra.rb:5
    Then I should see the saved details confirmed # features/chapter3/
steps/sinatra.rb:13


1 scenario (1 passed)
3 steps (3 passed)
0m0.064s


$ bin/cucumber -r features features/chapter3/sinatra.feature
Feature: Using Capybara and Selenium-Webdriver to Interact with Sinatra
App


  Scenario: Complete Book Review                        # features/chapter3/
sinatra.feature:3
    Given I am on a book review site                    # features/chapter3/
steps/sinatra.rb:1
    When I submit a book review                         # features/chapter3/
steps/sinatra.rb:5
```

```
    Then I should see the saved details confirmed # features/chapter3/
steps/sinatra.rb:13

1 scenario (1 passed)
3 steps (3 passed)
0m4.079s
```

> Because Capybara starts your application, this means you do not need to set the base host using `Capybara.app_host` or use full URLs in your calls to the `visit` method. You can simply use the relative path to the page such as `visit '/form'`.

Which driver to use and when?

It is important to understand that even when we have Rack::Test available, it may not always be the best option. As mentioned previously, using the Rack::Test driver will test your application's full stack and will run tests quicker than using any browser-based solution headless or otherwise. However, there are two important considerations:

- Rack::Test is not a real browser
- Rack::Test does not run any of your client-side code

It is important to bear in mind that there are features of a web server and browser that will affect the behaviour of the application under test which we will not be testing when using Rack::Test. For example, HTTP caching headers are not in play, so there is still a case for testing in this context.

> Rack::Test does maintain a cookie JAR, so the behavior of cookies should still be replicated as with a real browser.

Finally, and perhaps most importantly, Rack::Test is not going to test any of your application's client-side JavaScript as it deals only with code that runs on the server. If you have a Rails or Sinatra application that is entirely dependent on JavaScript and static assets to provide core functionality, you will need to ensure this is covered by your Capybara tests that use Selenium WebDriver.

As a rule of thumb it would be advisable to harness the power and performance of Rack::Test for running full stack tests that validate the core of your server-side integration. In addition, always ensure you have at least a set of sanity or smoke tests that you run using Selenium WebDriver in a real browser.

Capybara helps you here; if you are using Cucumber, simply tag scenarios requiring JavaScript support with `@javascript` and in RSpec put `:js => true` in your specs as in the following example:

```
#For Cucumber
@javascript
Scenario: Complete Book Review

#For RSpec
describe "Book Review"
  it "lets the user submit a review", :js => true do
```

Capybara will then swap out the drivers as required. If you don't want to use Selenium WebDriver as your JavaScript driver, you can change this to another driver such as Capybara-WebKit using `Capybara.javascript_driver = :webkit`.

A note on Rails/RSpec and Capybara

If you use Active Record within your rails application to manage database transactions, you may or may not be aware of the concept of **Transactional Fixtures**. The principle here is that when using compatible test frameworks, the database will be cleared between each test case ensuring there is no pollution between tests.

This code is part of `ActiveRecord::TestFixtures` and can be enabled or disabled in the test framework you are using.

Transactional Fixtures will work fine when your test framework is running within the same process as your application, such as when you are using Rack::Test with Capybara. However, as soon as you run your application in a web server and use a driver such as Selenium WebDriver or Capybara-WebKit, your tests start running in a different process and therefore have no visibility of the code running in the server. Hence transactions won't be rolled back after each test.

In this instance, what most people do is use Database Cleaner (`https://github.com/bmabey/database_cleaner`) to ensure the database is truncated between each test. The project's README will give you plenty of help in setting this up should you choose this option.

Summary

Capybara supports testing of Rails, Sinatra, and all other Rack applications out of the box and this support is a central part of the library.

We have covered what "Rack compatible" actually means and this is crucial to understanding why Capybara in conjunction with Rack::Test is so well suited to testing applications using Rails or Sinatra.

Finally, we considered which driver to use and when, highlighting that sometimes you will still need to use Selenium WebDriver to test some of your application's functionality. Clearly where JavaScript is concerned, Rack::Test will be of no use and you will have to use the Selenium driver.

Remember the "fail fast" mantra though, and use Rack::Test to run fast full-stack tests before you bring out the heavy guns of Selenium.

If your application is JavaScript heavy, don't worry, we are going to see how Capybara handles this with ease in the next chapter.

4
Dealing with Ajax, JavaScript, and Flash

It has been a long time since web applications consisted of mainly static HTML. Most modern web applications have huge amounts of JavaScript that modify the DOM on the client (in the browser). Automating such applications requires an additional level of awareness on the part of the developer authoring the tests. JavaScript in the DOM is not synchronous; event handlers are used to alter and modify the page as it loads and as users interact with it, and as such, our tests need to be robust enough to handle this asynchronous behavior.

Thankfully, Capybara was built with this principle at its core, so that makes things pretty easy for us. In this chapter, we will work through examples that demonstrate this.

We will also consider elements on the page that appear at first sight to be impossible to automate, such as flash components or HTML5 elements, for example, the `canvas` tag.

Ajax and asynchronous JavaScript

If you are not overly familiar with JavaScript or its role within the web application, a brief overview may be worthwhile.

JavaScript interpreters exist in all modern web browsers and allow developers to add client-side functionality to their pages by changing content dynamically once a page has loaded.

The API exposed via JavaScript is largely event-based, so JavaScript code running in the page can register to listen to a specific event and provide a function that will get called when that event occurs. An example of this might be a search input with an autosuggest feature, where JavaScript will listen for keypress events and then start to update the page with search suggestions based on the text input by the user.

Ajax (Asynchronous JavaScript and XML) is just a subset of the API available via JavaScript and relates to the ability to load content across the network asynchronously using XML or JSON (JavaScript Object Notation).

Why is this problematic for automation?

Basic page load is detected by most automation tools out of the box. For example, Selenium knows when the DOM is ready and won't allow interaction with the page until this has occurred. However, Selenium cannot know how your specific application's JavaScript will modify the DOM, and so this responsibility falls on you as the developer of the test.

Fortunately, Capybara has built in a wall of defense against this issue that removes as much of the brittleness from our tests as possible.

Capybara and asynchronous JavaScript

Let's look at precisely how Capybara helps us manage asynchronous JavaScript in our applications.

The following code snippets first show some simple markup from a web page and then some JavaScript that loads pictures from Flickr using Ajax and appends them as image tags to the existing markup.

Here, the `body` part of the document shows the initial state of the DOM prior to the button being clicked and the JavaScript being executed:

```
<body>
  <div id="main">
    <input type="button" id="load" value="Load Images" />
    <div class="section">
      <div id="images"></div>
    </div>
  </div>
</body>
```

And here is the JavaScript that loads the images and appends them to the document:

```
<script>
  $(document).ready(function() {
    $('#load').click(function(){
      var flickerAPI = "http://api.flickr.com/services/feeds/
      photos_public.gne?jsoncallback=?";
      $.getJSON( flickerAPI, {
        tags: "capybara",
        tagmode: "any",
        format: "json"
      })
      .done(function( data ) {
        $.each( data.items, function( i, item ) {
          $( "<img/>" ).attr( "src", item.media.m )
          .appendTo( "#images" );
          if ( i === 3 ) {
            return false;
          }
      });
    });
  });
</script>
```

The rendered page would look like the following screenshot:

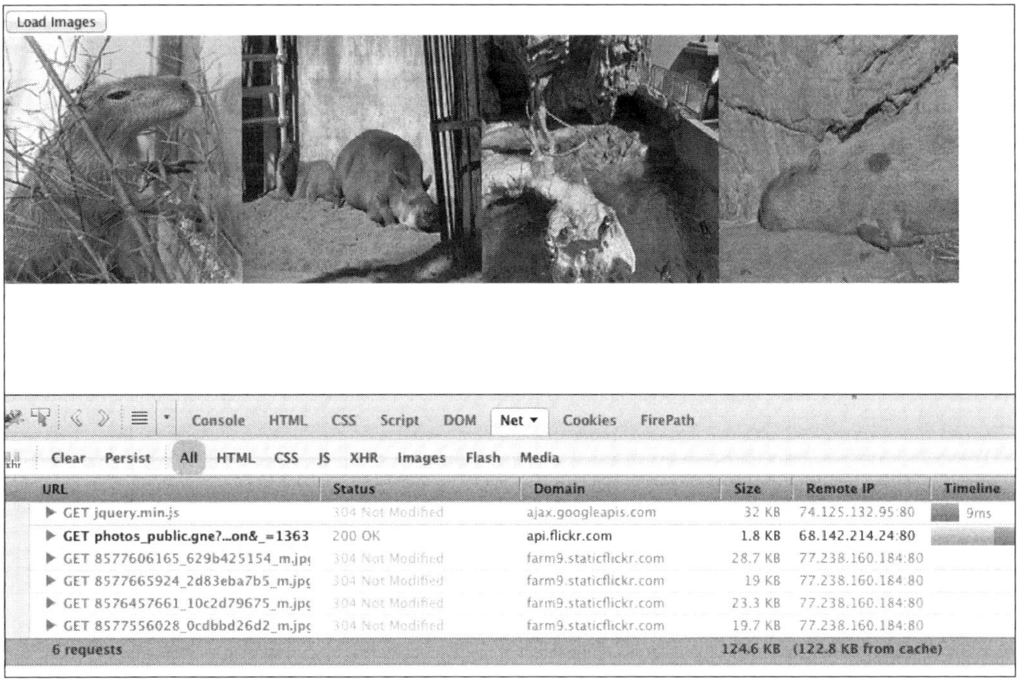

In this example, the Ajax request is made using the jQuery library (`http://jquery.com/`) and has been done using JSONP (JSON with Padding), which allows us to make a cross-domain request for data.

When a user clicks on the **Load Images** button, this causes four network requests to be made to the Flickr API to ask for images tagged with `capybara`. You can see these requests in the Firebug (`http://getfirebug.com`) console as shown in the preceding screenshot. This is completely asynchronous, so when we are testing "outside in" using Capybara and Selenium there is no way of knowing when these requests will complete.

Let's assume we have already completed a step that tells us to click on the **Load Images** button, and we now want to write a test to check that the four images have been loaded and added to the page.

```
Then(/^I should see all the images load successfully$/) do
  find(:xpath, '//img[4]')
end
```

> The preceding `xpath` expression checks for the four `img` elements. This is also possible with CSS3; to do so, include the following code:
>
> ```
> find('div > img:first-child:nth-last-child(5)')
> ```

Incredibly, that's all you need to do. You might assume that this wouldn't work because our test will simply load the page and then check for four image elements that would probably not be there, as the browser is still loading them.

Thankfully, Capybara builds retry logic into much of its API, so that we do not need to worry about doing it ourselves.

The amount of time which Capybara will retry defaults to two seconds, but can be overridden by setting the `default_wait_time` attribute; if you are using Cucumber, you can add this to your `env.rb` file:

```
require 'bundler/setup'
require 'capybara/cucumber'
require 'rspec/expectations'


Capybara.default_driver = :selenium
Capybara.default_wait_time = 10
```

It is important to note that these asynchronous retries only apply where the driver you are using supports JavaScript. For example, when using Selenium, these will most certainly work. If the driver doesn't support JavaScript, there is no need for Capybara to wait, as waiting for page load is sufficient.

Methods that handle asynchronous JavaScript

Having seen how Capybara's retry logic works when using a simple find, you now need to see how far this extends across the API.

Both Capybara's finders and matchers wait for asynchronous JavaScript.

Finders

You have encountered the finder methods earlier in this book and all of these methods have the built-in wait functionality.

As shown in the previous example, `find (:xpath, '//img[4]')` waited for sufficient time to allow the asynchronous JavaScript to run and for the browser to load the images. The other finders that have this capability are:

- `find_field`
- `find_link`
- `find_button`
- `find_by_id`
- `all`
- `first`

Matchers

The matchers that are used to validate content on the page will also wait for asynchronous JavaScript; for instance, to use an RSpec Matcher, you could change the previous example as follows:

```
Then(/^I should see all the images load successfully$/) do
  page.should have_selector(:xpath, '//img[4]')
end
```

As with the finder methods, you get this behavior for free with all the matchers and also with their negative counterparts as follows:

- `has_xpath?` / `has_no_xpath?`
- `has_css?` / `has_no_css?`
- `has_content?` / `has_no_content?` (Similar to `has_text?` / `has_no_text?`)
- `has_link?` / `has_no_link?`
- `has_button?` / `has_no_button?`
- `has_field?` / `has_no_field?`
- `has_checked_field?` / `has_no_checked_field?`
- `has_unchecked_field?` / `has_no_unchecked_field?`
- `has_select?` / `has_no_select?`
- `has_table?` / `has_no_table?`

Gotchas

Despite Capybara's powerful asynchronous defense mechanisms, it is still possible to be caught out. Let's look at another example:

```
<html>
  <head>
    <title>Asynch Examples
    </title>
    <script src="http://ajax.googleapis.com/ajax/
    libs/jquery/1.9.1/jquery.min.js">
    </script>
    <script>
      $(document).ready(function() {
        var addText = function() {
          $('.section').attr('style', 'visibility:visible;');
        }
        setTimeout(addText, 5000);
      });
    </script>
  </head>
  <body>
    <div id="main">
      <div class="section" style="visibility:hidden;">
        Capybara Rocks
      </div>
    </div>
  </body>
</html>
```

This page has some JavaScript code that runs at least five seconds after the page has loaded and sets the visibility style on the `div` with class `section` to `visibility:visible`. This makes the text **Capybara Rocks** visible to the user.

You might think that the following code would work and wait for enough time to check that the element becomes visible:

```
Then(/^Capybara waits for the element to be visible$/) do
  find('.section').visible?.should == true
end
```

In this example, Capybara will not wait for the element to become visible. The reason is that Capybara simply waits for an element with the correct class to exist within the DOM then immediately checks the visibility of the element and returns. This is because the `visible?` method is not one of Capybara's finders or matchers; it is simply a method used to query the state of an element at any given time.

You could get this behavior if you desired by writing your own custom `wait_for` method:

```
require 'time'

def wait_for(wait = 8)
  timeout = Time.new + wait

  while (Time.new < timeout)
    return if (yield)
  end
  raise "Condition not met within #{wait} seconds"
end

When(/^I visit a page that makes an element visible with a delay$/) do
  visit 'http://localhost/html/asynch.html'
end

Then(/^Capybara waits for the element to be visible$/) do
  wait_for(10) { find('.section').visible? }
end
```

The `wait_for` method accepts a wait time in seconds as an argument and then executes any block that is passed to it. It then continually runs the block, until either it returns `true` or the timeout value is exceeded.

If you find yourself in this situation, it is probably worth considering whether you could use a method or selector which does take advantage of Capybara's built-in wait functionality. For example, you could pass an additional parameter to the `find` method to ensure it waits for the element to be visible:

```
Then(/^Capybara waits for the element to be visible$/) do
  find('.section', :visible => true)
end
```

Capybara's API is so elegant that using this is almost always going to be a better option than the code that you might attempt to write in order to deal with such issues.

Flash and HTML5 – black box elements

Just as the use of asynchronous JavaScript and Ajax has pushed the boundaries of web applications, there are other components outside of static markup that make testing modern web applications challenging.

Examples of such components include:

- Flash applications, such as games, video players, and so on
- HTML5 `canvas` tag used for drawing using a JavaScript API
- HTML5 `video` / `audio` tag

All these components have something in common, that is, they have functionality that operates to some extent outside of the context of the DOM. We cannot inspect their internals using the techniques we have discussed so far, because all these techniques are based on inspecting the DOM for specific elements, their attributes, and text values.

For example, your application might dynamically draw pie chart diagrams on a canvas based on some user input and you would, of course, like to test this. However, when you inspect the DOM, all you see is the following code:

```
<canvas id="org_chart" width="500" height="500"></canvas>
```

This is because there is nothing you can inspect as the browser is rendering a bitmap dynamically based on the instructions passed via the JavaScript API.

You want to test these components using Capybara, but the issue here is not Capybara; you need to expose a testable API from these components to enable any browser-automation tool to stand a chance of adding value.

Flash

Flash applications are no different than some of the HTML5 elements. They are black boxes containing compiled code and embedded in the page. The only way to make a Flash application on your page accessible to test tools is to ensure you and your development team builds in a testable API that is exposed via JavaScript.

Flash allows this by offering the External Interface API (`http://help.adobe.com/en_US/FlashPlatform/reference/actionscript/3/flash/external/ExternalInterface.html`), whereby an ActionScript function can be made available to JavaScript. Additionally, you can use FlashVars (`http://helpx.adobe.com/flash/kb/pass-variables-swfs-flashvars.html`) to pass data into the embedded object from JavaScript or via attributes on elements.

From a test automation perspective, there is little difference in principle between a Flash component and some of the black box HTML5 components. In the following examples, HTML5 is used rather than Flash, so that you don't need to concern yourself with compiling ActionScript or building SWF files, which is well outside the scope of this book.

Exposing a testable API

The HTML5 `audio` element is another example of a black box component, similar to a Flash video player.

Imagine that your development team wants to embed an audio player into the pages of the site, choosing the HTML5 `audio` element around which to build the player. Initially, they are just going to build out some custom controls; later, they intend to add more advanced features such as user-defined playlists and linking to artist websites from the current track.

The team's initial spike just introduces the following custom controls:

- Play
- Pause
- Seek

As the team member responsible for test automation, you are left scratching your head; how can you possibly test that clicking on play actually plays the song and pause stops it? Though the native controls are visible, you cannot interact directly with these, as they are part of the Browser Object Model (BOM) and not the DOM.

The following page demonstrates how a very naive implementation of this might look:

```
<!DOCTYPE html>
<html>
  <head>
    <title>HTML5 Examples</title>
    <script src="http://ajax.googleapis.com/ajax/libs/
    jquery/1.9.1/jquery.min.js">
    </script>
    <script>
      $(document).ready(function() {

        $('#play').click(function(){
          $('audio')[0].play();
        });

        $('#pause').click(function(){
          $('audio')[0].pause();
        });

        $('#seek').click(function(){
          var val = $('#seekval').val();
          $('audio')[0].currentTime = val;
        });

      });
    </script>
  </head>
  <body>
    <div id="main">
      <input type="button" id="play" value="Play" />
      <input type="button" id="pause" value="Pause" />
      <input type="button" id="seek" value="Seek To:" />
      <input id="seekval" value="" />
      <div class="section">
        <audio src='http://www.vorbis.com/music/
        Hydrate-Kenny_Beltrey.ogg' controls="true">
        </audio>
      </div>
    </div>
  </body>
</html>
```

This example writes out an HTML5 `audio` element into the page, with a `src` element pointing to the file we want to play.

> The previous example uses jQuery (hence the use of `$`) to assist with finding elements and attaching events. This was deliberate for brevity and also because a lot of the teams you work with will be using jQuery. Of course there is no dependency here; you could just have easily used functions such as `getElementById` and `getElementsByTagName`.

There are buttons for **Play**, **Pause**, and **Seek To**, which use callback functions to hook into the JavaScript API for the `audio` element to play, pause, or seek through the song.

This page might look something like the following screenshot when rendered in the browser:

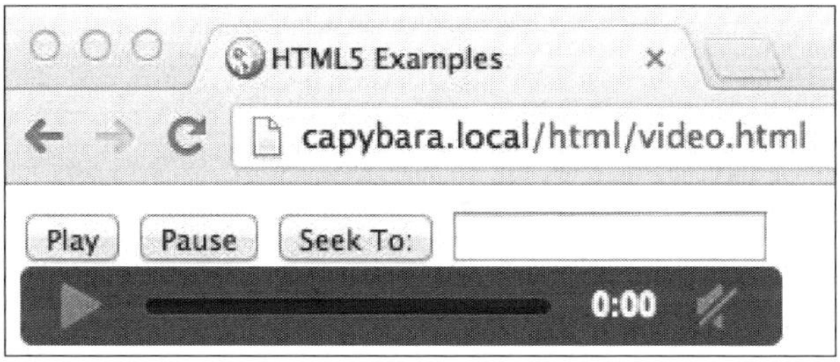

It is worth noting again that you can't interact with the native controls (at least not without some seriously unpleasant techniques), so how do you validate the behavior of your custom buttons and controls?

Not all hope is lost, and in fact, it turns out to be quite straightforward. Looking closely at the HTML5 audio specification reveals there are events that are raised by the browser when specific behavior is invoked. We can tap into these events, and all of a sudden, this behavior becomes immediately testable.

Test pages – behold the power!

If you come from a test background, you typically lean towards always wanting to test the application just as a user would use it and you may not be comfortable with taking a component out onto a test-specific page rather than testing it "in situ".

I can sympathize with this thinking; but often it makes sense to pull a component out, especially where it is an isolated piece of page, as with our audio player example. You will still want to write a thin layer of tests with it embedded in a real page. But to really put it through its paces, it will help to isolate it. The reason for doing this is that we can tap into all the JavaScript events, output some debug information into the page, and then use Capybara to scrape this information and validate that it is correct.

Let's update our example with some information gathered from events raised and then output these onto the page.

Additional elements are added to the markup, which will contain the current player state and song position:

```
<body>
  <div id="main">
    <input type="button" id="play" value="Play" />
    <input type="button" id="pause" value="Pause" />
    <input type="button" id="seek" value="Seek To:" />
    <input id="seekval" value="" />
    <div class="section">
      <audio src='http://www.vorbis.com/music/
      Hydrate-Kenny_Beltrey.ogg' controls="false">
      </audio>
    </div>
    <div>Player State: <span id="log">stopped</span></div>
    <div>Song Position: <span id="time">0.00</span></div>
    </div>
</body>
```

The JavaScript code then needs to be augmented to populate these new elements:

```
<script>
$(document).ready(function() {

  var updateState = function(state) {
    $('#log').text(state);
  };

  var updateTime = function() {
    var currTime = $('audio')[0].currentTime;
    var currTime = Math.round(currTime*100)/100
    $('#time').text(currTime);
  };

  $('#play').click(function(){
    $('audio')[0].play();
  });

  $('#pause').click(function(){
    $('audio')[0].pause();
```

```
    });

    $('#seek').click(function(){
      var val = $('#seekval').val();
      $('audio')[0].currentTime = val;
    });

    $('audio')[0].addEventListener('playing', function() {
    updateState('playing'); }, false);
    $('audio')[0].addEventListener('pause', function() {
    updateState('paused'); }, false);
    $('audio')[0].addEventListener('timeupdate', function() {
    updateTime(); }, false);
  });
  </script>
```

Now that the three `addEventListener` function calls have been added to the `audio` element, this information can be outputted onto the page using the elements with the IDs `log` and `time`.

Now your page contains debug information which you can use to test the behavior of the custom controls using Capybara:

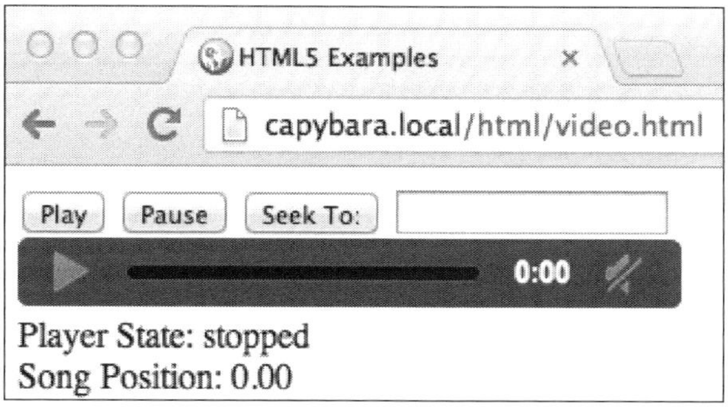

Since we have invested the effort to develop a testable page, the actual automation using Capybara/Selenium is straightforward. An important takeaway here is that although there is a trade-off by testing the component on a dedicated page, it makes our test automation a lot less brittle, as the test simply needs to be concerned with clicking on the buttons and scraping text, simple!

Our feature and steps might look something like the following:

```
Feature: Validate Custom Controls on HTML5 Audio Player

  Scenario: Validate 'play' control
```

```
    Given I visit a page with a custom HTML5 audio player
    When I click to play a song
    Then the song plays
```

```
Given(/^I visit a page with a custom HTML5 audio player$/) do
  visit 'http://localhost/html/html5.html'
end

When(/^I click to play a song$/) do
  click_on 'Play'
end

Then(/^the song plays$/) do
  find('#log').should have_text 'playing'
end
```

It should be obvious now that you can very easily add tests for pause and seek scenarios. In doing so, you will have made a previously untestable component perfectly testable.

Testing components "in situ"

There may still be occasions where testing a component in isolation on a dedicated test page is not appropriate, and all testing needs to be done against the page that is going to implement the component. In the example of the audio player component, you are unlikely to have the option of outputting the event information onto your actual applications pages.

Thankfully, we still have options for exposing the events that make the component testable, although it will mean your test code will not be quite as clean or maintainable; that's the trade-off.

When using Capybara with Selenium (and other supported drivers such as Capybara-WebKit), you have the option of executing arbitrary JavaScript against the current page. For example, the following line of code would get all the `div` elements on the page:

```
page.evaluate_script('document.getElementsByTagName("div")')
```

As a potential solution to your issue with exposing debug information on a real application page, you could agree with the team to change the application code and create JavaScript objects in the page with this information attached. To do this for the HTML5 audio example, the JavaScript would just need to be amended as follows:

```
<script>

var audioDebug = {
  state : 'stopped',
  time : 0.00
};

$(document).ready(function() {

  var updateState = function(state) {
    audioDebug.state = state;
  };

  var updateTime = function() {
    var currTime = $('audio')[0].currentTime;
    var currTime = Math.round(currTime*100)/100;
    audioDebug.time = currTime;
  };

  $('#play').click(function(){
    $('audio')[0].play();
  });

  $('#pause').click(function(){
    $('audio')[0].pause();
  });

    $('#seek').click(function(){
      var val = $('#seekval').val();
      $('audio')[0].currentTime = val;
    });

    $('audio')[0].addEventListener('playing', function() {
    updateState('playing'); }, false);
    $('audio')[0].addEventListener('pause', function() {
    updateState('paused'); }, false);
    $('audio')[0].addEventListener('timeupdate', function() {
    updateTime(); }, false);
});
</script>
```

In the preceding code, the `audioDebug` object is created to hold the debug information when the events fire. Since polluting the global namespace in JavaScript is discouraged, you will want to create this object within the namespace of the application's JavaScript code.

The Cucumber steps can now be amended to reflect this new strategy:

```
Given(/^I visit a page with a custom HTML5 audio player$/) do
  visit 'http://localhost/html/html5.html'
end

When(/^I click to play a song$/) do
  click_on 'Play'
end

Then(/^the song plays$/) do
  wait_for do
    page.evaluate_script('audioDebug.state').should == 'playing'
  end
end
```

The only difference is that you now run some JavaScript using Capybara's `evaluate_script` method that gets the `state` property from the `audioDebug` object.

> You will have to employ the custom `wait_for` function that was discussed earlier. As Capybara does not build in any kind of wait when executing arbitrary JavaScript, the likelihood is that if you click on **Play** and immediately check the state of the `audioDebug` object, it will not have had time to update its state.

When you discuss such strategies with your team, you might find that the developers could think of some clever abstractions to manage JavaScript events in the application. For example, you could implement a pattern that pushes the events into a proxy object and then have different strategy objects that can be switched on/off and determine what is done with the data; for example, whether the data is written to a debug object or it is written to the console for logging. It goes without saying that you will want to switch off this debug output when the application is deployed in production.

Summary

Dealing with asynchronous JavaScript is inevitably going to be a challenge you have to face. We saw how Capybara makes this easy by implementing built-in waits into all the methods that involve finding something on the page or interacting with elements which may not be immediately visible.

Additionally, we took on the challenge of testing black box components and used a HTML5 audio player as an example. We also saw that the most common approach to solving this problem is to expose a testable JavaScript API and, if possible, to implement test-specific pages with the debug output displayed on the page ready to validate using Capybara.

5
Ninja Topics

In the final chapter of this book, it seems appropriate for us to look beyond the basic API and functionality that Capybara offers. You now have all the skills required to automate your application using Capybara, regardless of whether it is a Rails/Sinatra application or a web application written using any other framework.

This chapter will ensure that you are comfortable using Capybara outside of Cucumber. It will also show how you can access functionality in your chosen driver that is not mapped by Capybara's API and introduce you to some of the other drivers that you may not have encountered.

Specifically, we will cover:

- Using Capybara outside of Cucumber
- Advanced interactions and accessing the driver directly
- Advanced driver configuration
- The driver ecosystem—some alternative options

Using Capybara outside of Cucumber

So far, most of the examples in this book have been set in the context of Cucumber step definitions, as this is by far the most common way in which people use Capybara.

However, Capybara is by no means coupled to Cucumber, and can be used in any setting you wish, within Test::Unit, RSpec, or just from vanilla Ruby code. In fact, if you are using Cucumber but want to abstract some logic out of your step definitions and into Page Objects, then you will still need to consider how to use Capybara outside of Cucumber's world (`https://github.com/cucumber/cucumber/wiki/A-Whole-New-World`).

> The Page Object pattern is a simple way of structuring your test framework if you are dealing with browser-based applications. You simply model each page (or each major UI component) as an object. Aspects such as CSS selectors can be stored as properties, and you can implement methods to manipulate the page. *Simon Stewart*, one of the lead developers on the Selenium WebDriver project, provides some useful best practices if you choose to implement this pattern, which are available at `https://code.google.com/p/selenium/wiki/PageObjects`.

Including the modules

The first option you have for using Capybara outside of Cucumber is to include the DSL modules into your own modules or classes:

```
require 'capybara/dsl'
require 'rspec/expectations'

Capybara.default_driver = :selenium

module MyModule
  include Capybara::DSL
  include RSpec::Matchers

  def play_song
    visit 'http://localhost/html/html5.html'
    click_on 'Play'
    find('#log').should have_text 'playing'
  end
end

class Runner

  include MyModule

  def run
    play_song
  end

end

Runner.new.run
```

In the preceding example, one of the tests from *Chapter 4, Dealing with Ajax, JavaScript, and Flash*, which verified the behavior of an HTML5 audio component has been re-written. Instead of using Cucumber scenarios, we have implemented our own module and class to run the test.

It is important to require the Capybara DSL file, as this contains all the Capybara methods that need to be "mixed in". In this example, we have our own Ruby module and crucially within this, the relevant Capybara module `Capybara::DSL` is included. In addition, the `RSpec::Matchers` module has also been included, which allows us to utilize standard RSpec Matchers (obviously you do not have to use RSpec; you could choose a different way to assert behavior). If you follow this pattern in your own code, you can now mix in any of the standard Capybara methods into your own module or class methods.

> It is worth remembering that if you include modules in a base class, then all subclasses will inherit the ability to use those module methods. This would come in handy, for example, if you were using a Page Object pattern, where the only class that would have to include the DSL module would be the base page.

Using the session directly

The other option for mixing Capybara into your code is to use the session directly, that is to say, you instantiate a new instance of the `session` object and then call the DSL methods on it.

The following example implements the same test as before, but this time by using a `session` instance and raising a simple exception if the expected content is not found:

```
require 'capybara'

session = Capybara::Session.new :selenium
session.visit('http://localhost/html/html5.html')
session.click_on 'Play'
raise 'song not playing' unless session.find('#log') == 'playing'
```

If you are using an object-oriented model for building your tests, you will need to pass the `session` instance around or find an appropriate strategy to deal with this, as you do not have the benefit of the modules mixing in the DSL methods globally.

Capybara and popular test frameworks

Capybara provides out of the box integration with a number of popular test frameworks; this is not a subject we will cover in depth, simply because they are covered very well in the Capybara README, which can be found at `https://github.com/jniklas/capybara`.

Cucumber

Throughout this book, examples have been set in the context of Cucumber, so you should be happy with how to implement Capybara's API in step definitions and do some simple setup in the `env.rb` file, such as setting the default driver. There are a couple of additional pieces of functionality that Capybara adds when using in conjunction with Cucumber, which are worth examining.

The first is that Capybara hooks into Cucumber's `Before do` block as follows:

```
Before do
  Capybara.reset_sessions!
  Capybara.use_default_driver
end
```

Apart from setting the default driver, this crucially makes a call to `reset_sessions!`, and this in turn will invoke some code in the underlying driver. In the case of Selenium, this deletes all cookies to ensure that you start each scenario with no pollution from the previous one. For `Rack::Test`, this will destroy the browser instance, so a new one gets created each time; for any other drivers, you will need to check the implementation of the `reset!` method to see what they do.

Finally, Capybara also hooks into any Cucumber scenarios you have tagged with `@javascript` and automatically switches you to the driver you have set up to handle JavaScript. For example, you may use `Rack::Test` as your default driver, but have set the following in your `env.rb` file:

```
Capybara.javascript_dirver = :selenium
```

In this case, any scenarios tagged with `@javascript` will result in Capybara starting a browser using Selenium as the driver.

RSpec

Outside of Cucumber, RSpec is one of the most popular Ruby test frameworks, lending itself well to unit, integration, and acceptance tests, and used inside and outside of Rails.

Capybara adds the following features to RSpec:

- Lets you mix in the DSL to your specs by adding `require 'capybara/rspec'` into your `spec_helper.rb` file
- Lets you use `:js => true` to invoke the JavaScript driver
- Adds a DSL for writing descriptive "feature style" acceptance tests using RSpec

For more details on these features, check out the README, which is available at `https://github.com/jniklas/capybara`.

Test::Unit

If you are using Ruby's basic unit test library outside of Rails, then using Capybara simply means mixing in the DSL module via `include Capybara::DSL`, as you saw earlier.

As noted in the README, it makes a lot of sense to reset the browser session in your `teardown` method, for example:

```
def teardown
  Capybara.reset_sessions!
  Capybara.use_default_driver
end
```

If you are using Rails, then there will be other considerations, such as turning off transactional fixtures, as these will not work with Selenium; again, the Capybara README details this behavior fully.

MiniTest::Spec

MiniTest is a new unit test framework introduced in Ruby 1.9, which also has the ability to support BDD style tests.

Capybara does not have built-in support for MiniTest, because MiniTest does not use RSpec but rather uses its own matchers. There is another gem named `capybara_minitest_spec` (`https://github.com/ordinaryzelig/capybara_minitest_spec`), which adds support for these matchers to Capybara.

Advanced interactions and accessing the driver directly

Although we have covered a great deal of Capybara's API, there are still a few interactions that we have not addressed, for example, hovering over an element or dragging elements around.

Capybara does provide support for a lot of these more advanced interactions; for example, a recent addition (Capybara 2.1) to methods you can call on an element is `hover`:

```
find('#box1').hover
```

In Selenium, this results in a call to the `mouse.move_to` method and works for both elements using CSS's `hover` property or JavaScript's `mouseenter` / `mouseleave` methods. Other drivers may implement this differently, and obviously in some it may not be supported at all, either where JavaScript support is non-existent (`Rack::Test`) or rudimentary (Celerity).

You can also emulate drag-and-drop using the following line of code:

```
find('#mydiv').drag_to '#droplocation'
```

Again, driver support is likely to be patchy, but of course this will work fine in Selenium WebDriver.

Despite all the bells and whistles offered by Capybara, there may still be occasions where you need to access the API that exists in the underlying driver, but that has not been mapped in Capybara. In this instance, you have two options:

- Call Capybara's `native` method on any `Caybara::Element`, and then call the driver method
- Use `page.driver.browser.manage` to call the driver methods that are not called on elements

Using the native method

If you wish to call a method in the underlying driver, and that method is one that is called on a retrieved DOM element, then you can use the `native` method.

A good example is retrieving a computed CSS style value. Elements in the DOM can obtain CSS properties in a couple of ways; firstly, there is the **inline style**:

```
<p style="font-weight:bold;">Bold Paragraph Text</p>
```

This information could be easily retrieved by accessing the `style` attribute via the methods we discussed in *Chapter 2, Mastering the API*. The other way in which an element obtains CSS properties is via `style` elements or stylesheets that are referenced via `link` tags in the page. When the browser loads the stylesheets and applies styles to the specified DOM elements, these are known as **computed styles**.

Capybara has no direct API for retrieving the computed style of an element, which was most likely a deliberate design decision as only a few drivers would ever support this. However, Selenium WebDriver does have this capability, and it is possible that you would want to access this information.

Consider the following code, where we apply a CSS `hover` property to a `div` element, so that when the user hovers over the element, it changes color.

```
<html>
  <head>
    <title>Hover Examples</title>
    <style>
      .box {
        height: 200px;
        width: 200px;
        margin: 10px;
        background-color: blue;
      }
      .box:hover {
        background-color: green;
      }
    </style>
  </head>
  <body>
    <div id="main">
      <div id="box1" class="box">
      </div>
    </div>
  </body>
</html>
```

The Cucumber step definitions that follow use Capybara and Selenium WebDriver to assert that the color has changed:

```
When(/^I hover over an element whose color changes on hover using
CSS$/) do
  visit 'http://capybara.local/html/chapter5/hover.html'
  find('#box1').hover
end

Then(/^I see the color change$/) do
  find('#box1').native.style('background-color')
  .should == 'rgba(0, 128, 0, 1)'
end
```

Here, the `style` method within Selenium WebDriver is accessed via Capybara's `native` method, and the value can then be validated.

> This highlights an important issue worth considering when checking computed styles. Different browsers may report the styles differently; for example, some may report a color as a hexadecimal code and others as rgba code; this could make your tests fragile when running across different browsers.

Accessing driver methods using browser.manage

The other use case is when we wish to access functionality provided in the underlying driver that is neither mapped by Capybara nor related to a specific element on the page.

A good example of this is accessing cookie information. There has been a long running debate on the Capybara forums and GitHub issue tracker, about whether Capybara should expose an API for cookie getters and setters, but the overriding feeling has always been that this should not be exposed (arguably, you should not set cookies in your tests, as this is changing the state of the application as a user never would).

Nevertheless, it is something you may well need to do, and given that Selenium WebDriver and a number of other drivers support this functionality, you will need to access the driver methods directly.

Consider this page that sets a cookie using JavaScript:

```
<html>
  <head>
    <title>Cookie Examples</title>
    <script>
      document.cookie = 'mycookie=foobar';
    </script>
  </head>
  <body></body>
</html>
```

The following steps simply visits the page and then outputs to the console all the cookies that are available on the current page:

```
When(/^I visit a page that sets a Cookie$/) do
  visit 'http://localhost/html/cookie.html'
end

Then(/^I can access the cookie using Selenium$/) do
  puts page.driver.browser.manage.all_cookies
end
```

We can access any method in the underlying driver by using `page.driver.browser.manage`, and then the method we wish to call; in this instance, we call Selenium WebDriver's `all_cookies` method, and the output will be as follows:

```
 [{:name=>"mycookie", :value=>"foobar", :path=>"/html/chapter5",
:domain=>"localhost", :expires=>nil, :secure=>false}]
```

Selenium WebDriver exposes a full API for accessing and setting cookies. The documentation can be found at `http://rubydoc.info/gems/selenium-webdriver/0.0.28/Selenium/WebDriver/Driver`.

Advanced driver configuration

So far, we have only set the default driver or the JavaScript driver using a symbol:

```
Capybara.default_driver = :selenium
```

It is quite likely that you will need to fine-tune the configuration of your driver or register multiple configurations, which you can select from at run time.

An example of this might be that you are running tests from your office, and the corporate network sits behind an HTTP Proxy (the bane of a tester's life). If you are using Selenium WebDriver with Firefox, you could register a custom driver configuration in Capybara as follows:

```
Capybara.register_driver :selenium_proxy do |app|
  profile = Selenium::WebDriver::Firefox::Profile.new
  profile["network.proxy.type"] = 1
  profile["network.proxy.no_proxies_on"] = "capybara.local"
  profile["network.proxy.http"] = "cache-mycompany.com"
  profile["network.proxy.ssl"] = 'securecache-mycompany.com'
  profile["network.proxy.http_port"] = 9999
  profile["network.proxy.ssl_port"] = 9999
  profile.native_events = true
  Capybara::Selenium::Driver.new(app, :browser => :firefox,
  :profile => profile)
end
Capybara.default_driver = :selenium_proxy
```

This configuration uses the Selenium WebDriver API to construct a custom Firefox profile, set the proxy details programmatically, register the driver with the name `:selenium-proxy`, and then make it the default driver.

Obviously the possibilities here are endless, and in browsers such as Firefox and Chrome, the amount of options you can customize runs into hundreds, so knowing how to set these is important. For example, you could use this technique to create profiles with JavaScript disabled or Cookies disabled to ensure your application behaves correctly in these cases.

> If you want to find out more about how to use different browsers and customize their settings using Selenium WebDriver, the documentation on the Ruby bindings is the most useful resource (`https://code.google.com/p/selenium/wiki/RubyBindings`).

The driver ecosystem

Capybara bundles two drivers, which as you know are Rack::Test and Selenium WebDriver. However, Capybara is architected in such a way to make it easy for developers to implement other drivers, and indeed, there is a healthy ecosystem of pluggable drivers, which offer interesting alternatives to the two built-in options.

Capybara-WebKit

Pretty much every developer I know who is passionate about test automation is desperate for one thing—a headless browser with great JavaScript support. A headless browser is one that runs without a UI. Headless browsers typically run tests faster than opening a real browser, and make it easy to run in Continuous Integration (CI) environments, where often, a windowing environment (either MS Windows or X11 on Linux) may not be available.

You can refer to the following links to find out more about Capybara-WebKit:

- `https://github.com/thoughtbot/capybara-webkit`
- `http://qt.digia.com/`

Capybara-WebKit is a driver that wraps QtWebKit and is maintained by the guys at Thoughtbot. The Qt project provides a cross-platform framework for building native GUI applications, and as part of this, it provides a WebKit browser implementation that lends itself to headless implementations.

There is a slight catch with this particular implantation of QtWebKit; you will need to install the Qt system libraries separately, and there is still a reliance on X11 being present on Linux distributions despite the browser being headless.

Poltergeist

Poltergeist is another driver, which, in the background, will use QtWebKit. The difference here is that it wraps PhantomJS, which brings a couple of potential advantages over Capybara-WebKit.

You can refer to the following links to find out more about Poltergeist:

- `https://github.com/jonleighton/poltergeist`
- `http://phantomjs.org/`

You will still need to install PhantomJS as a system dependency, but the PhantomJS project has tackled some of the issues around making QtWebKit purely headless, so you will not need X11, and you will not need to install the entire Qt framework, because PhantomJS bundles this for you.

Capybara-Mechanize

Mechanize is a headless browser implemented purely in Ruby, and has long been a stalwart for the Ruby community; it uses Nokogiri at its core to provide DOM access, and then builds browser capabilities around this.

You can refer to the following links to find out more about Capybara-Mechanize:

- `https://github.com/jeroenvandijk/capybara-mechanize`
- `https://github.com/sparklemotion/mechanize`

Capybara-Mechanize is a driver that allows you to use Mechanize to run your tests. It is a very powerful option, but there are some important aspects to consider, such as:

- **No JavaScript support**: Mechanize does not contain a JavaScript engine; therefore, none of the JavaScript on any of your pages will be run
- **No rendering engine**: Mechanize does not contain a rendering engine; therefore, no computed styles will be evaluated
- **Fast**: Because it's not attempting to evaluate JavaScript and do graphical rendering, it will be super fast

The benefits of using Mechanize may not be obvious at first sight, and a lot will depend on how your site is implemented. For sites whose functionality is wholly dependent on JavaScript, this option is clearly not feasible; however, if your site follows the principles of "progressive enhancement", where JavaScript is simply used to enrich the user's experience, Mechanize is a great option. You can implement all the core functional tests using Mechanize, which will be ensure they run with minimal latency and will be far less fragile than using Selenium, and then just implement a sprinkling of Selenium or WebKit tests to test the JavaScript dependent features.

Capybara-Celerity

The final driver that is worth considering is Capybara-Celerity, which wraps the Ruby library Celerity. This is especially worth a look if you are running your test code on JRuby (Ruby running on the JVM) as Celerity itself wraps the Java library HtmlUnit.

You can refer to the following links to find out more about Capybara-Celerity:

- `https://github.com/sobrinho/capybara-celerity`
- `https://github.com/jarib/celerity`
- `http://htmlunit.sourceforge.net/`

Going back a few years, HtmlUnit would have been a serious consideration for anybody wanting a headless browser, indeed it was the default headless browser for the Selenium WebDriver project. HtmlUnit is a pure Java implementation of a browser and uses Rhino (`https://developer.mozilla.org/en/docs/Rhino`) to run JavaScript. Unfortunately, you may find that the JavaScript support still fails when attempting to evaluate heavy-weight JS libraries, as the project is not actively maintained, and keeping pace with the demands of modern browsers is unrealistic for a small project.

If you are looking for a headless alternative to Mechanize, Celerity is worth a look, but don't rely on it for JavaScript support.

Summary

This chapter has taken you from confidently implementing Capybara tests against your application to being a Capybara ninja.

By understanding how to use Capybara outside the comfort zone of Cucumber, you can now use it in almost any setting and even write your own custom framework. This is important even if you use Cucumber, because as your Cucumber tests grow, you will probably want to implement some Page Objects and mix `Capybara::DSL` into these.

Another important aspect of writing effective tests is being able to configure the underlying driver and access it directly when required; there is nothing magical about this, and it means you can harness the full power of your chosen driver.

Finally, we introduced some alternative drivers that should whet your appetite and prove why Capybara is such a powerful framework. You write your tests once and then run them in multitude of compatible drivers. Win!

Index

U

V

W

X

Y

Thank you for buying

Application Testing with Capybara

About Packt Publishing

Packt, pronounced 'packed', published its first book "*Mastering phpMyAdmin for Effective MySQL Management*" in April 2004 and subsequently continued to specialize in publishing highly focused books on specific technologies and solutions.

Our books and publications share the experiences of your fellow IT professionals in adapting and customizing today's systems, applications, and frameworks. Our solution based books give you the knowledge and power to customize the software and technologies you're using to get the job done. Packt books are more specific and less general than the IT books you have seen in the past. Our unique business model allows us to bring you more focused information, giving you more of what you need to know, and less of what you don't.

Packt is a modern, yet unique publishing company, which focuses on producing quality, cutting-edge books for communities of developers, administrators, and newbies alike. For more information, please visit our website: `www.packtpub.com`.

About Packt Open Source

In 2010, Packt launched two new brands, Packt Open Source and Packt Enterprise, in order to continue its focus on specialization. This book is part of the Packt Open Source brand, home to books published on software built around Open Source licenses, and offering information to anybody from advanced developers to budding web designers. The Open Source brand also runs Packt's Open Source Royalty Scheme, by which Packt gives a royalty to each Open Source project about whose software a book is sold.

Writing for Packt

We welcome all inquiries from people who are interested in authoring. Book proposals should be sent to `author@packtpub.com`. If your book idea is still at an early stage and you would like to discuss it first before writing a formal book proposal, contact us; one of our commissioning editors will get in touch with you.

We're not just looking for published authors; if you have strong technical skills but no writing experience, our experienced editors can help you develop a writing career, or simply get some additional reward for your expertise.

8887157R00060

Made in the USA
San Bernardino, CA
25 February 2014